MW01258339

FATAL HOLIDAY

A True Crime Story

by Judy Gigstad

NEW FORUMS

Stillwater, Oklahoma
U.S.A.

NEW FORUMS PRESS INC.

Published in the United States of America
by New Forums Press, Inc.1018 S. Lewis St.
Stillwater, OK 74074
www.newforums.com

Library of Congress Cataloging-in-Publication Data Pending

This book may be ordered in bulk quantities at discount from New Forums
Press, Inc., P.O. Box 876, Stillwater, OK 74076 [Federal I.D. No. 73
1123239]. Printed in the United States of America.

ISBN 10: 1-58107-168-X
ISBN 13: 978-1-581071-68-9

Contents

Author's Note

The following book is a true crime story which, without the help of many supportive people, would not have been written. I have deferred to the wishes of some who did not want their names published. To respect their privacy, fictitious names for all children under the age of eighteen have been used.

The information in this book comes from interviews, personal experience, public records and extensive notes taken in the courtroom. An occasional paraphrase does not compromise statement intent. Certain facts reported in the story come from actual trial testimony.

I thank the members of my writers' group, *The Dead Writers Society*, who encouraged me to write the book because of my unique involvement. Special thanks go to my mentor, Carolyn D. Wall, whose careful editing produced a cohesive story from a tangle of words. My daughter-in-law, Sarah Gigstad, was my secretary in the courtroom when I could not attend proceedings. Without her copious notes, much testimony would be missing. Thanks also to Sharon McKay, who provided numerous photographs used in the manuscript. Dwayne Blakely and Glenda Lee contributed photographs as well.

Homicide detectives, Roland Garrett and Gary Damron, then Oklahoma County District Attorney, Wes Lane and prosecutor, Gayland Gieger were generous with their time when interviewed. I thank the friends and acquaintances of the Andrew family who were kind enough to spend time with me.

I dedicate the story to my husband, Dean, for his enduring support.

J.K.G.

CHAPTER ONE

An Invasion

On Tuesday, November 20, 2001, the intruder mouthed a silent thanks for a sixty-degree Indian summer day. He slipped into the garage from an adjacent storage space that was enclosed by a surrounding eight-foot stockade fence. The last rays of sunlight faded to dusk a few minutes past 5:30 p.m. Shadows lowered, dropping in a moderate breeze. His timing for this mission must be precise; his partner demanded attention to detail.

A beam through the slightly open door gave him sufficient light. Head to toe dark clothing helped him blend into the dingy garage, and the stage was set for action. Long matchsticks, burned and extinguished, lay scattered in front of the massive furnace close to the door between the kitchen and garage.

A wine-red Chrysler mini-van was parked alongside the east wall. The intruder inched into the narrow space near its front end and crouched beside the cold headlamp. Time to check weapons.

He pondered. What if the target wouldn't take the bait? Would three shots be enough? The shotgun held only one round. But he was a marksman and up to the task. He'd eject the first shell with lightning speed if a second was needed. His partner would be positioned beside the furnace, situated to fire at close range. He'd laid a 22-caliber pistol on the mini-van's hood, ready to be grabbed for the second shooting.

He fumbled with the black ski mask he wore. To avoid the victim's recognizing him; he would draw the tight knit fabric down over his face. He'd shove it into a pants pocket afterwards. His partner has taken care of the remaining escape details; carefully selected route and door openings.

It had been years since he'd felt the adrenalin flow in anticipation of such a covert action. Heat coursed, limbs tensed. The rush was on. Crouching, he waited for the victim's arrival and the action to begin. Like his days in the army, he was prepared for victory. His team would prevail.

— — — — — — — — — — — — — — —

Packed suitcases sat in the front hallway of the home at 6112 Shaftsbury Rd. At six o'clock, Robert Andrew would pick up his children for the long Thanksgiving holiday. He was ready for a vacation, an old-fashioned holiday in Enid with his parents and his three brothers' families. He'd even agreed to take Gen's new puppy along, despite the additional bother of a cage and dog food. These few days would be the first extended weekend with his kids since the preliminary divorce settlement. After Thanksgiving he and Brenda would alternate holidays. When he turned his black Nissan into the entry to their street, Rob groaned. Even rows of green roofline lights shined bright against the house's newly painted mahogany exterior. Christmas lighting before Thanksgiving seemed like a sacrilege. He'd call Ronnie. Ron always helped him set things in perspective. Rob punched in the number on his cell phone. The answering machine beeped and Rob left a message.

"Hi, buddy. I'm ready for a great time with my kids. I'm on my way to pick them up. Hope you have a good holiday, too. I'm turning down the street now. The garage door is going up. Looks like they're coming out now. Catch you later...."

His soon-to-be ex-wife, Brenda met him at the doorway. Her brown hair shone tawny in the green glow of the Christmas lights. Rob's breath caught at her dazzling good looks. It always did. Why couldn't they work out their differences and spend all the future holidays together?

Brenda broke the spell. "You can take their stuff through the garage to the car. It'll be easier, with the dog's cage and all. I need you to check the pilot light on the furnace. It's out and it won't stay lit."

He asked, "Where are the kids?"

"Watching TV in my bedroom. I'll get them after you light the furnace."

"Okay."

Rob Andrew opened the trunk of his car and entered the shadowy garage.

The marksman hiding behind the minivan was ready. Showtime. His target knelt in front of the furnace, one knee resting on a spent matchstick, his hand reaching for a fresh one. Boom! A single shot tore through Rob's stomach, into his side.

The woman screamed, the sound echoing and carrying out of the garage. At the same time, blood gushed from the victim's side. He groped for something to stop the flow, grabbed a black trash bag filled with tin cans and used it as a shield. While Rob swayed forward, then collapsed, the shotgun burned its first spent shell upward toward the ceiling. The gunman loaded a second round and handed the weapon to his partner.

Boom! The shotgun blasted again, like a wildfire, the fragments of Rob's life exploding in its furious wake. The woman's second scream was a deafening wail in the fading afternoon. A third blast ripped into her upper arm.

She staggered and managed another scream, then moaned when she saw her wound, blood trickling onto her pink sweater and down her forearm. She fell to her knees beside her husband who lay in a pool of blood. Instinctively, she fumbled for her phone and dialed 911.

"Hi...I've been shot. My husband's been shot."

The dispatcher spoke, "Okay, calm down, ma'am. Who shot you?"

"I-I don't know. They had on black masks...."

A job well done. The shooter had performed according to plan. He executed the escape route, disappearing into the enveloping dusk. The time was 6:15 p.m.

Screaming sirens announced police, emergency vehicles and ambulance-chasers. In minutes, yellow tape surrounded the perimeter of this violated cul-de-sac. Media vans could not access the site. On a curb by the driveway Brenda Andrew held her wounded arm against her body and rocked forward and back.

Rob Andrew would never celebrate another Thanksgiving.

CHAPTER TWO

A Bloody Night

Sitting in his Oklahoma City Police Department issue patrol car, Captain Roger Frost glanced at his watch. Nearly 6:00 p.m. and neighborhood activity appeared normal. He'd be glad for a day off by Thanksgiving on Thursday. For much of his thirteen-year career as a police officer he'd patrolled Lansbrook, an Oklahoma City neighborhood. On a cop's salary the additional income from the neighborhood watch helped.

About an hour ago, he'd written a traffic citation for a driver speeding at the intersection of Lansbrook Lane and Arlington. Routine. Nearby streets, including Shaftsbury, were the picture of normalcy, not even an open garage door, no gates standing wide. Not even a late autumn breeze to spoil the calm.

A 911 operator's voice startled him. The operator had talked to a Lansbrook resident on Shaftsbury. Frost flipped on the siren, spun the car in the nearest cul-de-sac and drove back to 6112 Shaftsbury, all within one minute of the 911 call. According to protocol, he secured the area in the case of a crime.

And a crime scene it was. Three more police officers arrived behind him. A man's body lay motionless on the floor of the garage at 6112. A woman slumped near the door to the home's interior, apparently wounded in the upper arm. A black Nissan sedan was parked in the driveway. Frost recognized the woman as Brenda Andrew. Usually perky, smiling and dressed like a model, she now was disheveled, her shiny dark hair strung across her face. Her blue jeans were spattered and streaked with blood and her pink sweater was stained where the bullet had entered her arm.

He guided her out of the garage and sat her on the curb. He'd need her to give him an accurate review of the crime, with descriptions of the suspects.

Traffic stops, an occasional vandalized mail box and a rare auto or home burglary were the extent of Lansbrook's criminal activity. On Frost's beat, gun shots were rare. This house was not in "the hood" where shots normally blasted the still of the night.

Quickly, Sergeant Warren, behind them, secured the garage and perimeter with yellow crime tape.

Frost asked Brenda. "How many of them were there?"

"Two men, with dark hair, wore black clothes."

"Can you tell me which way they went?"

"I think one was by the van and one was toward the Duncan's."

Brenda sighed and held her wounded arm. But she spoke calmly, in contrast to the frantic scene behind her. Paramedics had arrived and knelt in the garage, working to revive her husband.

Frost continued. "Did the gunmen say anything?"

".... Maybe six or seven words. I-I can't remember."

She turned back toward the house, scanning it. She looked worried. "I need to check on my children."

"Where are they?" Frost asked. "I'll go check. Can I take them somewhere? I need to get you to the hospital and have that arm looked at."

"The next door neighbor....Tom and Mary Ann Duncan," she said. "I don't want to go without my kids."

Behind them, Sergeants Ramsey and Warren had donned rubber gloves, had roped off the crime scene and were processing evidence on the floor where Rob lay. Brenda seemed oblivious to their operations.

In recent weeks Frost recalled that she had requested back-up police patrols. Ramsey and Warren had responded. In a difficult divorce situation, she'd feared trouble from her husband. Frost also had watched the home during his security shifts. Now, his job was to get answers.

"Ma'am, did either guy touch your husband after he was shot?" he asked.

"I think one of them grabbed the back of his pants." Brenda moaned again.

Frost signaled for the paramedics to attend her, stood and walked into the house. At first, Brenda had hyperventilated and required oxygen. The medics gave her no additional drugs. She'd said that the kids were in her bedroom watching TV, downstairs in the back of the house. He paused at the bedroom door, listening. The TV's volume was like a missile explosion. When he knocked and opened the door, Gen's eyes were fixed on the screen, and Connor was fast asleep. He gently moved them from the room, up the stairs and outside through the front door, skirting the garage. He led them around the outside of his parked patrol car and into the neighbor's front yard. Neither child asked a question. They seemed unaware of the commotion surrounding them. The EMSA workers had helped Brenda into their van and applied preliminary aid to her wound.

After he made sure the children were safe with the neighbors, Frost rode with Brenda to Baptist Hospital, hoping he'd acquire additional information. She knew him and would likely respond to his questions more comfortably than with strangers. At the hospital, she removed her bloody clothing and turned it over to detectives who had arrived. After her wound was treated and bandaged, officers drove her to police headquarters where she met with Detective Roland Garrett. She didn't seem bothered to be covered by two hospital gowns. Frost finished his report and turned it over to Detective Garrett.

Brenda appeared to be tired. "I need to check on my kids. I've asked my friend, Cindy Balding, to come and get them for the night."

She fiddled with the bandage on her arm, uninterested in recalling more details of the shooting, her thoughts elsewhere.

Detective Garrett suggested, "Please call me in the morning so we can talk some more, when you're rested."

"Okay," she replied.

A police officer drove her to the Balding house to join her children at around 2:30 a.m.

Cindy Balding, Brenda's friend and mother of Genesee's best friend, drove half a mile to the Shaftsbury cul-de-sac later in the evening on November 20. She took both kids from the Duncan's house, along with the new puppy and Connor's miniature dachshund. Both kids were engrossed in a board game with Mary Ann Duncan. After arriving at the Baldings, they played awhile, and then went to bed.

When Brenda arrived, she looked worn out.

"Do the children know about Rob?" asked Cindy.

"I'll tell them in the morning," Brenda said.

Early the next morning, Brenda was on the phone, first to her lawyer, next to her family. Cindy overheard Brenda say, "I can't believe you haven't heard the news." Concerned that Genesee and Connor would shatter on hearing about their father's death, Cindy was surprised at Brenda's cavalier attitude.

Behind closed doors, Brenda told her kids about the shooting. When they left the bedroom neither child showed any outward emotion. Cindy offered Brenda a change of clothes, but she refused and remained in the hospital gown. Later in the morning, Detectives Garrett and Damron dropped by to talk with Brenda again and took her back home.

She'd have to answer Rob's family's questions, then plan a funeral and pick up the broken pieces of their lives.

CHAPTER THREE

1930's ... A Tarnished Home

A house, like its residents, possesses unique personality. Child-like, it might whisper, "I've got a secret..." Chipped paint, knotted rafters and dented plaster tell its stories. Tragedy brands a home. Such a house exists in upper middle class Lansbrook, in Oklahoma City.

The sprawling oil-rich city outdistanced in square miles only by Miami, Florida, boasted peaceful suburban acreages. The Charles Urschel country estate was one of the town's perimeter jewels, complete with a rock garden and water-lily covered lake that enhanced its pastoral quality. In the 1940's, seven lakes, numerous bridges and Oklahoma's second swimming pool were its recreational benefits. Today, residents of Lansbrook still enjoy the ceramic tile-lined pool and original log bath house.

Before the land changed ownership, the Urschel family would know terror of enormous proportions. On a sultry July night in 1933, Urschel played bridge with his wife, Berneice and good friend W.R. Jarrett and his wife. The four sat on the Urshels' screened-in porch at their mansion in the center of the city.

Notorious outlaw Machine Gun Kelly and his partner, Albert Bates, burst onto the porch through a backyard gate, armed with a submachine gun and a six-shooter.

"Hands up! Which one of you is Urschel?" shouted Kelly.

When neither victim spoke up, the outlaws bound, blindfolded and gagged both men and forced them into the back seat of a waiting sedan. The kidnappers drove them to a hideout, the Shannon ranch in Texas. Jarrett was freed and directed to deliver a ransom letter to Berneice Urschel, demanding $200,000 for her husband's release.

Berneice notified the FBI. Ten days later, with the ransom paid, the kidnappers freed Urschel. Government agents later apprehended Machine Gun Kelly, who spent his remaining days in a federal prison. Urschel feared for his safety and retreated from notoriety to his sprawling country estate.

In 1944 the Urschels moved to San Antonio and sold the suburban property to an oil company that later became Pan-American Petroleum. Later, grown children of Pan-American's employees remembered lazy summer picnics on the rambling acreage. During Pan-American's ownership, the main house burned to the ground. The blinding smoke fogged the property with an eerie aura.

Nostalgia may have influenced real estate developer Dick Coyle when he purchased the land from Pan-American. He gave English names to streets in the development. *Lansbrook* means "brook running through the land." The 180-acre suburban addition became a multi-use residential plot, the city's first covenant community of 396 homes. Residents agreed to code restrictions, paid for security patrols and parks maintenance.

For the past three decades Lansbrook's children have explored its winding paths. Well-lit parks abound with tree-sheltered walkways that attracted young and upwardly mobile families, a child's playground paradise. My two sons built a tree house in the common greenbelt area, with wood pieces beside the trails. To their chagrin, a board member instructed them to remove the lumber. Neighborhood covenants forbade free construction.

In 1991, Lansbrook's elitist image was tarnished when a resident, Leroy Dennis, murdered his wife, burned the body and deposited her bones on his ranch property north of Oklahoma City. Dennis' twelve-year old son discovered the remains. His father told the boy that he'd unearthed possum bones. Detectives heard the story, arrested Dennis and sent him to trial. He was found guilty and is still in prison today. Headlines were splashed with details of the heinous crime. Lansbrook could not escape humiliation.

Shaftsbury Road was one of the last streets developed in the neighborhood. In its brief history, the house at 6112 was home to two families. Attempted robberies scarred both families, but each aftermath was different.

Paul Day was the house's first owner during the opulent oil boom of the late 1970s and early '80s. He owned and operated oil rigs in Texas, was hard-working and God-fearing, a rough man with unlimited generosity. He owned a vast firearm collection that he kept secured in two garage vaults. Day kept a pistol on top of a grandfather clock in the entry hall and a rifle behind the door, both armed. He hid a loaded pistol in his boot.

On one occasion the big man accidentally fired a rifle in the garage. The bullet slammed through the sheet rock and lodged in an exterior wall, near the living room fireplace. For many years the hole was visible. Day's teenage son gave the house a second blemish. Practicing his quick draw, the boy shot a hole in a wall mirror.

One Sunday morning while the Days were attending church, burglars attempted to steal the firearms. An earsplitting alarm startled the neighbors. When police arrived, they found no missing guns and that the thieves had been chased off by the noise.

By 1991, the economic climate of Oklahoma worsened. The 3,000 square- foot house at the end of the cul-de-sac sold. Its new owners, Robert and Brenda Andrew, moved into Lansbrook to raise their young daughter, Genesee. Three years later they welcomed a son, Connor. Like the Days, the Andrews were committed to home, family and church. Unlike their predecessors, they owned but a single gun, a coming-of-age shotgun given to Rob by his father. Rob stored it in his closet. Unlike the oilman, he was not fond of firearms.

The house was branded.

While the Andrew family lived in Lansbrook, the place was burglarized once. Thieves took cash and jewelry that included a large-carat diamond ring and an expensive camera. The crime was never solved. The Andrews' insurance covered the loss, a new security system was installed and life went forward. But a cloud lingered on Shaftsbury. The ultimate insult would be inflicted on November 20, 2001. If the house had a voice, it would plead, "Stop the misery!"

CHAPTER FOUR
A Precious Flower

The state of Oklahoma has a rich history from the blast of the gunshot that instigated its settlement until now. Located in northwest Oklahoma, more than 20,000 of the first 100,000 people into the Cherokee Strip remained in "O" County, later known as Garfield County. Its town of Enid was established as the county seat. Supposedly, a group of hungry cattle drovers rode into the settlement and the *DINE* sign designating the cook tent was mysteriously turned upside down to read, *ENID*.

As the result of a dispute over the location of a postal site, two town sites were established. A North Enid post office competed with that of Enid. The town became a center for commerce for all of northwest Oklahoma and has evolved into the "Bright Star of the Great Plains." Vance Air Force Base, wheat farming, cultural development in the arts and regional health services mark its progress into the twenty-first century. Oil and gas exploration in the area thrust Enid's economy into a first-class small city.

Don and Rose Evers married on April 19, 1958 settling in Garber, Oklahoma, north of Enid. In 1961 their first child, Kim, was born, a blond, blue-eyed daughter whom they loved and nurtured. Two years later, Rose gave birth to a second daughter, Brenda. Unlike Kim, Brenda had darker skin that suntanned easily, bright dark brown eyes and a spunky personality. The two girls clashed in normal childish rivalries and loved the parental attention they drew.

When John Jay was born six years later, the sisters included the new baby in their circle of love. However, before John Jay entered his first year of school, disaster struck the Evers. Rose took her son to the doctor for the required round of inoculations before entering public school. A diptheria-pertussis-tetanus shot turned his arm fiery red, and sore. High fever, delirium, nausea and seizures marked the following days. Rose nursed him back to health with remedies at her disposal, but her boy would never fully recover. He'd suffered brain encephalopathy, leaving him mentally and emotionally retarded. His intellectual development would not exceed that of a six-year-old.

As the children grew up, Kim and Brenda protected their little brother, supporting him with constant attention. Riding bicycles in the streets, they'd wait for John to catch up. He didn't move fast enough on one morning's outing and was overtaken by a Doberman. Defending its invaded territory, the dog snarled and gnashed its teeth. Brenda, saw the danger and turned her bike. She grabbed John and snatched him up. At a young age, she displayed strength beyond her years, both emotional and physical. Together, the sisters sheltered John against a harsh world. The Evers threesome left an imprint on Garber's history.

Years later, relatives would recall warm and funny memories they shared with the Evers children. Paul Southwick was a first cousin on the Evers side of the clan. He remembered times when the cousins would spend an overnight. Brenda had an infectious laugh and would entertain them all with her antics. She'd cackle when her father filled a huge griddle with pancake batter for a group breakfast. Paul later referred to her as a "precious flower, a beautiful person."

The Evers girls' label of ..."good girls" was marred by only an occasional prank. Their mother recalled a time when Kim and Brenda were left alone with their water-color paints. Not to be outdone by Picasso, the girls brushed swaths of paint on one another. Rose discovered the entrepreneurs in time to mandate an on-the-spot cleanup.

Along with her cousins, Brenda displayed a penchant for drama. With Paul, the girls set the stage for an original presentation of the Daniel Boone story. Normally, Brenda took the role of Mingo, the dog, complete with canine sound effects.

Brenda's shared duties in shielding their brother limited her time for nurturing close friendships. However, she participated in varied activities. She was involved in church projects as well. The family belonged to the Immanuel Lutheran Church in Garber. Brenda helped with younger children in the annual summer Vacation Bible School. An excellent student, she earned straight A's in most of her high school classes and joined the cheering squad at Chisholm High School. Her elementary school attempts at drama paid off when she entered the *Miss Teenage America Pageant* in Edmond, Oklahoma. Although she didn't win, the experience lifted her self-confidence. Her high grade point average earned her a membership in the National Honor Society.

The pretty dark-eyed twirler drew attention from the boys in her class. By the time she graduated from Chisholm High School, Brenda had a rich collection of companions, both male and female. She became friends with Amanda Kelly at the summer church camp, Lutherhoma, where the two served as youth counselors. The following semester they shared a room at Southwestern Lutheran College in Kansas.

When Brenda's room number was set, Rose and Don Evers drove to the campus, loaded down with paint buckets, brushes and white chintz cloth. They worked to make their daughter's home-away-from-home a comfortable space. Soon the walls glistened with hot pink paint. Handmade white curtains with soft ruffles billowed on hot September days.

An hour's drive away, Rose Evers remained on call for her daughter. Brenda telephoned often for a fresh skirt or sweater to hang in her half of the small closet. Rose was happy to drive over to campus to solve her daughter's wardrobe problems. Her first college year finished, Brenda relaxed in Garber and worked on her suntan at the swimming pool in Enid.

That summer, she would make a friend who would change her life forever.

CHAPTER FIVE

A Jokester

Enid was home to the Andrew family as well as the Evers. Married in a local Baptist church in 1954, E.R. and Lou Andrew moved to Stillwater, where he enrolled at what was then Oklahoma A&M College. A degree in business prepared him for several early jobs in Colorado, Missouri, Kansas and finally back in Enid. By 1966, E.R. had founded the Andrew Real Estate Company. Lou later joined her husband in real estate, earned her license but never showed prospects a single property. She couldn't stand the idea of being told 'no.' However, she took over the company's bookkeeping and has continued that function until now.

On September 19, 1962, Robert Dale Andrew was the third son born to E.R. and Lou. Bill and Tim held the first and second places on the family tree. Several years later, Tom would be their fourth. Life in a small city in the heartland provided a stable environment. The Andrew family was rambunctious, fun-filled, spiritual and caring.

A favorite story from Rob's childhood was an occasion when he signed Christmas cards for the family.

His brother Tom quipped, "The dog signed them with an ink paw print."

Rob was not a graceful child. Sports were never his forte. But, early on, his good sense of humor came to the fore. To make matters worse, Rob had a wandering eye that caused him tremendous difficulty with depth perception. Both eyes needed correction. Reluctantly, he wore thick glasses.

His vision improved only to the point that thinner lenses created a more handsome image than his childhood "four eyes."

When the Andrews became our neighbors in Lansbrook, Brenda called me several times with a request to cut and save newspaper ads for discounts on glasses. She made certain that Rob's glasses wouldn't break their budget. He shattered or broke them all too often.

Rob was raised in the Southern Baptist church and held to its doctrine throughout his life. The Bible gave him strength and insight, and he lived each day following rich Christian principles. Like Brenda, his church background provided stability while growing up in the "flower child" '60s and early '70s. Religious beliefs guided his decisions.

Rob's good humor made him the jokester in his family. He filled household gatherings with hilarity. After he graduated from Chisholm High School in Enid in 1980, he decided to pursue a marketing degree at Oklahoma State University. The Bible had guided him; now a second book inspired him in business life, Dr. Seuss's Green Eggs and Ham. Both occupied prime spots in his library.

Summer was Rob's time for rekindling family ties during college. He remained close to his younger brother, Tom, who was still in high school. Tom worked as a lifeguard at an Enid pool and was a magnet for the girls who made daily visits to the pool. Dark-haired and handsome, Tom easily struck up conversations. Rob came to the pool occasionally to pick Tom up at the end of the day. Often, he arrived early enough to drop into the water for a swim.

One evening, Tom told him, "This dark-haired, good-looking chick at the pool's been asking about you...she wants to meet you."

The following day Tom introduced Rob to Brenda Evers. She was headed for a Lutheran-sponsored college in Kansas but she had an eye on Robert Andrew, his glasses not a deterrent.

After several years of courting, they married on June 2, 1984. The new Mrs. Andrew accompanied Rob back to Stillwater where he completed his degree in advertising, with a minor in marketing. She received her degree in business administration

During his first two years at the University, Rob joined organizations related to his major and exhibited the leadership skills essential to a stellar career in advertising. Other students in his field noticed a change, however, when he returned to school married to Brenda. They were friends with the tight-knit group of married students, but Rob's happy-go-lucky personality had mellowed and grown serious. Close friends in business societies noted the change. His quirky humor seemed absent.

Within two years, both Rob and Brenda were ready to enter the business world. He accepted a job in Texas, and with bright hopes they moved to the Dallas area. He worked hard to establish a reputation in advertising. Within a short time Rob had paid his dues, and the Andrews moved back to Oklahoma City when he accepted a position with Jordan Associates.

Brenda interviewed for and accepted a job with Bank of Oklahoma. She worked up to a position of Administrative Assistant in her nearly seven years of employment. Though diligent, she was surprised that, at the bank's Christmas party in 1987, she was selected as Employee of the Year and was presented with a plaque honoring her service. Brenda had been an asset to the bank, but she longed for something else, to be a stay-at-home Mom.

Meanwhile, Rob built a reputation at Jordan. His winning personality was a benefit to gathering a burgeoning list of clients for the company. Big names such as Disney, Blue Cross/Blue Shield and locally based giants joined his client stable. His energy and imagination opened new vistas to them. In their community the Andrews were a young couple on the financial and social rise.

CHAPTER SIX

New Neighbors

Paul and Linda Day had been friendly neighbors, their children now grown and with married lives of their own. Contracting with a builder, they had bought the house next door to ours, one of the first families to live on Shaftsbury. Three additional dwellings were occupied before we attended a builder's open house. Bee Jay Garrison had constructed a custom home on the corner next to his own house. We'd gone to the opening on a whim, never dreaming that we'd leave with a contract.

A gigantic bust in the economy hit Oklahoma City when Penn Square Bank failed in July, 1982. Both large and small oil companies were affected by the sudden drop in corporate profits. The larger companies could sustain moderate losses, taking time to build on inventories at hand, but small drillers and oil service companies suffered major hits and scores opted for bankruptcy. Paul Day was one of the unfortunate. For several years he played financial tag with his creditors. When he hired a tractor-trailer to load up two of the massive safes from his garage, his economic fall appeared unavoidable.

With a sad heart, I watched a "For Sale" sign hammered into the Days' front yard. We had felt close to this big man with an equally large heart. On Paul's deck Dean and I had spent hours listening to stories of the early Texas oil fields. Too soften their financial blow; Linda took a job at Dillard's in sales. She never complained. When the house sold, I felt as if a part of my family had broken away.

While the Days were active Church of Christ members, the new owners next door were Southern Baptists. I felt they would bring strong values to the cul-de-sac.

Our new neighbors, Rob and Brenda Andrew, had been blessed with a baby girl, Genesee. Brenda's hopes of quitting her job seemed close to reality. On occasion, we met Rob's parents who traveled from Enid on a visit. E.R. and Lou Andrew had raised four boys. We visited with them in the front yard on frequent trips to the city. Brenda's mother came to see the family but not as often as the elder Andrews. Then, in the mid-nineties, I remarked to Dean that we hadn't seen Rob's parents for a while.

Four years later, the Andrew family grew to include Connor. Both children were fair-skinned, like Rob, with light blond hair. Gen's eyes were blue, but Connor had inherited Brenda's deep brown. After Connor's birth, Brenda became obsessed with losing the excess weight she'd gained during her pregnancy.

Proudly she told me, "Rob let me buy a Nordic Track machine. But he doesn't want it to be seen in the living room. It folds up tight and I can keep it in the kitchen closet."

I thought that was odd, but didn't question her. Perhaps her husband was a neat freak. It wasn't long before the effects of her workouts were visible. Home from a shopping trip, she'd climb from her low-slung red convertible, showing a long, slender leg. Brenda looked stylish in the youthful attire of the times, miniskirts and jersey tops. Men on the street couldn't help but admire her, right down to her long black boots. She'd toss luxuriant dark brown hair, an attractive asset to her restored girlish figure.

Brenda was wholly engrossed in her children. Most days she drove the kids to school, untrusting of the bus system available. A shy child, Genesee trailed behind her mother if Brenda borrowed an ingredient for a baking project. Three closest neighbors received the benefit of Brenda's kitchen efforts. When she signed on as homeroom mother for Genesee's class, Brenda tried a recipe for cookies, brownies, muffins or bread on us. We were willing participants. She'd come to the door, holding a plate of goodies. "I'm not sure how this will taste. It's pumpkin bread," she'd say. Sampling the delicious bread, we questioned her lack of confidence.

If Brenda was aware that a neighbor was ill, she brought them a fresh pie or portion of a dinner. She even walked around the cul-de-sac with a neighbor diagnosed with Alzheimer's disease. When his symptoms worsened, his wife was nervous in trusting her husband to stray far from their house. Although he was old enough to be her father, Brenda was his friend. No doubt memories of caring for her brother inspired her.

Sadly, her own father died suddenly. Shortly before Don's death, Rose Evers had brought a shiny battery-powered toy car for Genesee's birthday. But Don hadn't come from Enid with her.

After the birthday celebration, I heard a commotion outside my door, in our backyard greenbelt. Genesee drove the little car as if she were on a busy freeway. Later, Connor raced it like a NASCAR driver.

On rare occasions, Rob wore a helmet and rode his bicycle in the Shaftsbury cul-de-sac, followed by both children also wearing helmets. While my boys had raced bicycles on greenbelt paths in and around the parks, the Andrew youngsters never ventured far from their own yard.

Rob did not own a reel lawn mower that was needed to cut the Sun Turf planted in his front yard, so Dean did the honors. True to his nature, Rob worked little out of doors. He did construct a sand box beside the deck in his side yard. Connor shoveled through the glistening white grains with toy tractors and animals.

The family's numbers grew when Connor received a baby rabbit. Excited by the responsibility, he talked Brenda into planting carrot seeds.

Brenda made no secret of the fact that she was not an animal lover. However, she purchased a puppy for Genesee, a female Maltese they named Casey. From an early age, Genesee had talked about growing up to be a veterinarian. Now, the little white dog yapped and brushed the patio pavement like a mop. Brenda griped openly about cleaning the messes.

"I'm not fond of dogs, but Genesee wanted one so bad that I gave in. Casey's small but she's still in the way. It's Genesee's job to feed and care for her."

The Andrews didn't get involved in neighborhood politics but blended well into its landscape. Rob's job kept him busy. He was climbing the corporate ladder and was awarded the title of Vice

President for his efforts. The downside of his commitment was that he spent exhausting hours working overtime.

Brenda would say, "Rob's a workaholic. He's always working."

True, on a Saturday morning, we saw Rob on the deck, poring over papers while sipping coffee. Working in our own yard, Dean would call out, "Hey, Rob, don't you get enough stress at the office?"

Rob would break into his broad smile. "Yeah, but it doesn't seem to wait."

Halloween was a special night for the family next door. Early in the evening both children, outfitted in costumes, pumpkin buckets in hand, rang our doorbell. Rob and Brenda stood behind them, prodding.

"Trick or Treat?" First they were timid, then less so.

We'd 'oooooh and ahhhhhh' over their costumes as if never having seen a ghost or witch so embellished. Brenda always bought showy garb for the occasion. Rob's grin explained his feelings. Halloween had been an obvious favorite holiday from his childhood. I always had a camera close by to record the moment.

Both children, especially Genesee, were shy around adults. Head bowed, with eyes downcast, she stood beside her mom. It bothered me that I couldn't break through to her with a kind word or question. Brenda often prodded her to speak or give me a "thanks." Halloween was the closest we came to a dialogue.

Once I overstepped my boundary as a neighbor, asking, "Rob, have you considered seeing someone professional about Genesee's shyness?"

He smiled but brushed me off. "She'll be okay when she starts school. Brenda was shy when she was a little girl. But thanks for asking."

I thought that his comment was odd. Brenda had always seemed outgoing to me. Best not to antagonize one's neighbor. Besides, it really wasn't my business.

While Rob worked long hours and traveled more often, Brenda's mom role increased when Genesee began to attend public school. She enrolled in dance classes and fell in love with ballet. Brenda shopped for the best studio. When ballet progressed to toe dance, Brenda went through the weekly ritual of twisting Genesee's hair into the ballerina's classic bun. She drove the red convertible in and out of the driveway on trips to the dance studio, to Brownie Scouts at school, then to Connor's soccer practices. One afternoon, she stepped out of a shiny, dark red Chrysler mini-van.

"I finally broke down and bought my "Mom-mobile," she told me. "Guess that's the *in* thing to have these days."

Now, she fit the suburban stereotype. Rob, not interested in the hassle of automobile shopping, gave Brenda sole responsibility for buying their cars.

Brenda seemed constantly on the go — to church, school, dance classes, grocery shopping, and endless activities.

CHAPTER SEVEN

New Rules

The Andrews' marriage went through a mini-crisis. Rob's passion for his work intensified; Brenda's loneliness increased. In 1994, Rob's traveling became routine. The children's activities took a large bite from Brenda's time, but a void had been created; jealousy ate at her. She wasn't sure if she resented the advertising agency or if Rob was having an affair with someone at work. There, on occasional visits, Brenda had met several cute young things, recent college graduates.

Rob was exhausted when he came home from work. The last thing he wanted was marital strife. He believed in a rigid code of marriage ethics and recorded his daily musings in a diary. He felt a strong marriage would grow from regular church attendance.

When the Andrews were new to the neighborhood, we held a casual conversation in the yard about church life. It seemed Rob's faith motivated his personal and professional activities.

"Where do you all go to church?" I asked. "Is Brenda still a Lutheran, like Dean?"

Rob smiled but was adamant. "I was raised a Southern Baptist. I believe that the *man's* preference rules the family. We belong to Village Baptist Church."

I had never heard such impassioned conviction. I stammered a brief acceptance and changed the subject. Rob's frivolous side was the facet that I had known. I was in unfamiliar territory. His declaration of faith was strong.

College activities consumed our own lives when both our sons attended Oklahoma State University, seven years apart. With both, we had gone back and forth to Stillwater for sporting events and fraternity gatherings. We didn't interact with the Andrews during those years except for the brief greeting on coming and going in our driveways. Our socialization with them was limited. But when Brenda wanted an opinion on dress, home decorating or needed a taster for baked goods, the door was open. If bickering made an inroad to ugliness in their marriage, it was not an obvious fact.

Much later, Brenda revealed that the two had had a temporary separation in 1994.

"Rob moved out for about a week," she confided. "He drove around in his car instead of sleeping on the couch or getting a place."

I was aghast. My face must have shown it.

She said, "We've had problems for a long time. I think he had an affair. Maybe we shouldn't have ever gotten married in the first place."

The separation was short-lived. Rob had moved back into the house, unnoticed by friends and neighbors. Brenda had put new rules in place. Rob's parents would be welcome upon her invitation, but not for spur-of-the-moment visits. We had missed seeing their car in the driveway.

The same was apparently true for *her* relatives. She'd not been close to her father during these years. Brenda had become uncomfortable with her young children being close to her brother, John. His size and apparent lack of physical control was part of her decision.

She had long ago told me, "I don't want my kids around my brother. My dad doesn't understand."

Brenda's protectiveness was a damper on her two young children. They appeared content playing video games, reading books and playing board games with the short list of friends who were allowed to come and play. Grandparent exposure had apparently become less important. Perhaps Brenda felt threatened by too much family and chose to keep the circle small.

I was sad for the children's sake. For me, close family ties were an important part of growing up.

CHAPTER EIGHT

Rumor Mills

Village Baptist Church housed one of the largest congregations in Oklahoma City. For more than a year, Brenda hoped that she could convince its governing board members to elevate Rob to a leadership position.

In the yard one afternoon, she remarked to me, "I'm going to petition the Church Elders to elect Rob a Deacon. He deserves it."

"How does that work," I asked.

"It's a lot of politics," she replied.

Rob's age may have worked against him toward the appointment. I heard no more about the idea. Before long, the Andrews changed their church affiliation to become charter members of a mission church in the northern Oklahoma City suburb of Deer Creek. North Pointe Baptist Church was the satellite congregation that Village Baptist started.

In 1999, the family was active in church life, with Rob joining the choir. He joked with fellow singers and made practice a lively event. He joined an early morning Bible study group and recorded his thoughts and concerns in a daily prayer journal. On occasion he shared his writings with Ron Stump, a North Pointe member who had become his best friend. Rob's religious faith deepened and he willingly shared it with others. He penned his idea of a perfect marriage, expressing optimism that Brenda would someday share in his dreams.

Brenda found her niche in the church family by teaching youth classes. On Wednesday evenings, Rob drove the children to North

Pointe for Youth Choir while he sang with the adults. Rob's faith grew more intense while Brenda followed a more social path within the congregation. She was friendly to visitors, encouraging membership in the small community. There, her social skills were an advantage.

The Andrews had not been members at North Pointe long when they were asked to participate in an outreach project in Brazil. Rob jumped at the chance to go, but Brenda elected to stay at home with the kids. The trip was open to non-church members and Rob invited a co-worker at Jordan Associates. Judi Brown had envisioned a humanitarian project like this one for years and was eager to join the group. She professed Christian values and shared her Bible-based beliefs with those of the missioners from North Pointe.

When they returned home, Rob was exuberant about his experience in Brazil.

Talking to us to us in the back yard, his face lit up.

"It was the most rewarding experience I've had," he said. "To be able to share Jesus Christ with those people was incredible. They'd never heard about Him and I could visit and tell them stories from the Bible and share the faith. Fantastic!"

Brenda's reaction seemed detached, especially when Rob talked about the girl who had gone with them. Rob had become better acquainted with her and he'd submitted Judi's name at work for a promotion. Her moral credentials were above repute. Rob's enthusiasm was effusive. He would gladly have repeated the experience of sharing the Word of God.

Family life settled to a normal pace until the Andrews returned home one evening to discover that someone had broken in. The master bedroom had been ransacked. An expensive pair of diamond earrings, valued at $10,000.00 was missing, along with a high-quality camera. Nothing else of value appeared to have been taken. Brenda called the police and filed a report.

With little evidence, the police were not optimistic. "Ma'am, the burglars left no fingerprints and it's difficult to know if we'll apprehend them. Give us the descriptions of the stolen items, and we'll watch for them to show up in confiscated contraband, or pawned merchandise."

Insurance coverage replaced Brenda's earrings, minus the deductible amount. She believed that Lansbrook security had let her down, and with indignation confronted the board member in charge of security.

"An officer is supposed to patrol this neighborhood regularly," she said. "He wasn't anywhere around on our street."

Officers soothed her, assuring her they would help apprehend the crooks. True, an occasional crime slipped through their security, but they had an outstanding prevention record. Cruising patrol cars were a detriment to high crime in the neighborhood. Brenda warned the neighbors to watch their possessions.

Rob and Brenda had been friends with young couples at North Pointe, several with children near the ages of Connor and Genesee. Besides Ron Stump, they socialized with oil and gas professional, Rick Nunley and his wife, Cindy. Brenda had worked with Cindy at the bank. The Nunley's daughter studied at Dynamo, the same gymnastics studio where Brenda took Genesee several times a week. While the girls were in class, their mothers often chatted and discovered common interests.

Rick Nunley worked long hours for Devon Energy, a growing oil and gas company. His hard work enabled them to make an upscale move into a suburban home near Edmond, Oklahoma, on Lake Arcadia

Brenda was excited, telling me about the Nunley's purchase.

"We're starting to house hunt too," Brenda told me one afternoon when she waved farewell to Cindy.

"We'd hate to lose you. You're such good neighbors," I replied. I'd gone out to the mailbox and now chatted with her. "Where are you looking?"

"We'd like to buy a house in Deer Creek, closer to our church," she said. "But my friends Rick and Cindy have a neat place at Lake Arcadia. That would be great, too."

"Have you found anything that suits you?"

Brenda frowned. "So far, Rob thinks Deer Creek is too expensive for us. He'd like to build an addition to this house. Maybe add an office from the other side of the garage, onto the storage area there."

I breathed a sigh of relief. I didn't like the idea of getting accustomed to new neighbors again. Our age difference limited close relationships, but the little family next door had become our friends.

On occasion, Dean and I were invited to parties on the Andrew's spacious deck. Although Rob would open a beer or drink wine at these events, we never saw him overindulge.

One evening, we were invited to join a small group for a cook-out on their deck. Rob confided that some good friends were getting divorced.

"Can you believe this?" he said. "The rumor around church is that I'm the cause of their breakup. I'm supposed to have had an affair with the wife. What a hoot."

Standing nearby, Brenda chimed in.

"Yeah, Rob supposedly had an affair with our friend, Cindy Nunley. She and Rick are getting divorced."

"Aren't those the people who live at Arcadia?" I asked.

"Yeah, but we'll still be friends," Brenda said.

Brenda certainly didn't lack friends, in or out of the church family. She supported Rick Nunley and consoled him during the divorce proceedings. On occasion, I noticed the Nunley car next door.

Each morning Rob left home at daybreak to participate in a Bible study group, then went on to the office. By the year 2000 at Jordan Associates, Rob's expertise and ingenuity had rendered him invaluable. His numbers had skyrocketed. Flying to California to service a Disney account, he'd stay overnight. Sometimes he'd drive to Tulsa to meet with an important client, accompanied by an associate from his office.

Rod Lott, a graphic designer and freelance writer, frequently rode with Rob on the trip to Tulsa. He'd admired his boss since the age of thirteen when Rob had worked as a summer intern at the Beals Agency that Lott's grandfather had owned. In 1995 Rod was an account executive at Blue Cross/Blue Shield. Rob had kept in contact with the kid from Beal's, no doubt remembering good times they'd shared. Rob literally stole Rod Lott from Blue Cross/Blue Shield and hired him at Jordan. The two called on the Tulsa account several times a week.

Rod had met Brenda only once before, in the parking lot at Office Depot. At that time he thought she was "nice, but a bit weird." Later, at Ad Club meetings, they socialized, but Rod soon discovered that Rob and Brenda were direct opposites. Brenda talked about the latest rumors at Rob's office, while her husband joked with his co-workers. Rod concluded that the couple was like mismatched socks. He felt uncomfortable around Brenda.

While Rob had worked at Dobson Communications before working at Jordan Associates, he'd hired Rod's wife Malena. He'd gone out of his way to come by the Lott's' place for a garage sale. He'd even visited Malena when both Lott children were born.

Meanwhile, Brenda continued her interest in office gossip. On a business trip to Jamaica, she confided in Malena.

"I've been having an affair," she said, matter-of-factly. "Rob only married me because I look good in a bikini. I think Rob's having an affair with a girl he works with anyway."

Neither Lott nor his wife believed Brenda's accusations.

"Rob would never have an affair with anyone," Rod said.

Brenda continued to obsess with the "workplace affair" idea. Later, she confided in me that Rob's "woman friend" from work would pick him up before sunrise on many a morning. She talked about the relationship as routine, but I detected an edge when she described watching Rob throw a briefcase in the backseat and drive off with a female co-worker.

While Rob traveled and expanded his authority at the company, Brenda spent increasing hours with good-looking, sandy-haired Rick Nunley. After Rick's divorce was final, he'd spend designated weekends with his children. Brenda offered help in the kitchen and with childcare. Once, she drove out to Rick's house to help his daughter bake a cake for a school project. Rick appreciated the attention and their friendship deepened.

Their encounters became sexual and took place at his house. At the same time, cavernous holes deepened in the relationship at the Andrew residence.

On the road, Rod Lott noted that Rob didn't end his cell phone conversations to Brenda with an "I love you…" He mentioned it to Rob.

"She says it makes her feel uncomfortable if I tell her I love her," Rob replied.

The marriage didn't appear on the firmest of bedrock to Rod. But he didn't pry further. None of his business. But he was concerned that the man he so respected in business was unsettled at home.

Brenda continued the affair with Rick but grew restless. The man lived at the opposite end of town. Finally, she called an end to their trysts.

I want to make things right with Rob," she said. "But we can still talk on the phone."

The telephone courtship continued for several years.

CHAPTER NINE

A Remodel

The Andrews could not agree on a possible move from the house on Shaftsbury. Rob tried to please Brenda, but her wish list was longer than he could fill. Her insistence on a new house became a wedge between them and a source of numerous arguments. Rob slept on the living room couch more than one night.

Brenda's grudging compromise was to remodel the house. Her first priorities were fresh coats of paint on the interior walls as well as stain and paint on the exterior. Brenda sorted through her lengthy list of friendships for a suitable contractor.

In November of 2000, Brenda shopped regularly for groceries at the Buy For Less grocery store, a couple of miles from Lansbrook. She liked the prices and fresh produce. Accompanied by her children after school, she'd drive there for weekly shopping rather than to the closer Albertsons or Homeland.

William "Stanley" Morgan worked at Buy for Less as a manager. He was a good-looking, well-built man in his late forties, over 6-foot tall, jet-black hair with a slight curl, a handsome man. He couldn't miss seeing the attractive young woman with two young children while she shopped the store aisles. Dressed in a miniskirt, Brenda flashed a wide smile at him the first trip past his station. She was vivacious, full of spunk and talked well beyond food item inquiries. Encouraged by her flirtations, his ego inflated.

Married for thirty-one years, he had fathered two boys, now both in their early twenties. For their entire marriage, Stanley had been faithful to his wife, Patricia. However, he couldn't stop fantasizing about Brenda. Each time she shopped, her necklines plunged lower, and hemlines rose shorter. She told him she was married.

"My husband abuses me emotionally, mentally," she said.

He sympathized, and the flirtation continued.

Three weeks later, she handed him a motel key. "You've passed the test," she said. "Meet me there at two o'clock this afternoon. I'll be waiting for you."

The motel was close to the store, near the Olive Garden Restaurant on Northwest Highway. True to her word, and minus her children, Brenda waited there for him. She displayed a voracious sexual appetite. For him, the sex was fantastic. She was without guilt, repeatedly insisting that her husband mistreated her. Rob's abuse, she said, had killed her desire for sex with him.

From early December, 2000 until May, 2001, a torrid affair continued between Brenda and Stanley. They met twice weekly, in the afternoons. She insisted on paying for the motel rooms. At his insistence, and as an ego boost, Stanley paid for the room once or twice. Their sexual encounters never took place at Brenda's house. Stanley had access to both her home and cell phone numbers and dialed them daily. For secrecy, they devised a code to identify him as the caller on her cell phone.

On one afternoon, eagerness charged them to begin foreplay in Brenda's car. Like adolescents pushing moral decency, their fondling led to the sex act in her back seat.

Brenda told Stanley about remodeling her house. He'd done some part-time painting and offered to give her a price for the job. His sons also would be available in the summer, once classes at Oklahoma University had ended. She wanted both interior and exterior walls painted. Together with a possible backyard deck rebuilding, the job could amount to nearly $20,000.00.

In late winter, Stanley began painting the inside of Brenda's home.

She called me over one afternoon. "I can't decide what color to paint the front hallway," she said.

I looked at her choices. The swatches ranged from burgundy to crimson. Color coordination was not her strong point.

"Are you sure that you want to go that deep?"

"Yes, dark walls are the *in* colors everywhere," she said.

She settled on a blood red shade that I considered garish. But it was *her* house.

By May, the sexual relationship between Brenda and Stanley had begun to fade. During an afternoon tryst at the motel, she told him, "You've changed. This isn't fun any more. I want to end it."

Stanley was relieved. Although their sex hadn't diminished, cheating on his wife bothered him. But he needed the additional income that Brenda's painting job gave him. They decided to end the sex acts but to remain friends, and he'd continue the remodel. Finishing the hallway at her house, he moved into the dining room with buckets and brushes. Even working part-time at this job, the task was demanding.

Rob hadn't been around during the daytime hours when Stanley painted. To Stanley, Brenda insisted that she hated her husband. He didn't question her feelings. The elusive husband appeared to be a workaholic, up and gone for work at sunrise and never home before dark.

When the interior walls were finished, she asked him to bid on the deck. They agreed on a reasonable sum and construction began. The old deck had rotted beyond repair. Stanley ordered new lumber, with plans to add short fencing between the Andrews' side yard and our house. I expressed regret to Dean.

"I don't want a fence hooked to our house. It'll look tacky."

"Brenda wants a short fence there to keep kids and dogs in her yard," he said. "You'll see. It will look nice."

"Her kids don't play outside. Have you ever seen the dog go out, except to pee?"

Brenda had her way. The slats were spaced with light between, an open look. I begrudged the concession but admitted that it looked better than I had anticipated. Stanley installed a second gate at the back of the deck, opening to the stairs behind the house that led to the greenbelt. The overall effect was tasteful.

Stanley finally met Rob Andrew when he began work on the deck. Early, on Saturday mornings, Rob read the newspaper and drank coffee there. The two chatted and Stanley was puzzled about the picture Brenda had painted of her husband. The smiling man who talked about the home remodeling was friendly and witty. Stanley disagreed with Brenda's portrait of a brutal man and questioned whether he abused her emotionally. This guy couldn't hurt a fly.

In the seventy-five or more times he had come to the Andrew home to work, Stanley also observed Brenda's other male friends. When they had begun the affair, she'd come into Buy For Less with her friend, Rick Nunley. She wanted the two to meet. It was important to her that her friends like one another. The clandestine relationship she had had with Nunley was over, she assured Stanley. However, she talked about her husband with malice.

"I've stayed with Rob for his money," she said.

"Why don't you divorce him, work part-time and be rid of your husband?"

Brenda's expression turned dark. "How dare you suggest that I would leave my children and have to get a job? That's not acceptable. I just wish he was dead. I could have all the money and go on with my life."

Stanley didn't share her hatred of Rob. He felt sorry for the guy. He figured she'd get over it eventually. He did not bring up the divorce again, didn't want to sour his job status with Brenda. Besides, she had brought home a new friend that spring, one from the church. An insurance agent named James Pavatt.

"My friend Jim is *just* a friend," Brenda insisted.

Jim watched Stanley hammering and sawing on the deck and talked about his own background.

"I was in top-secret work for the government, a professional killer in my former life." He bragged, "I've killed in the past, but I only missed once. I can't tell you the details."

Stanley thought the conversation odd. Jim was much shorter than he, with a slight build. The guy looked to be in his late forties, his thinning hair tinged with grey, in sharp contrast to Stanley's dark hair and good looks. Maybe the guy felt intimidated by Stanley's size and muscular build. In addition, Jim talked non-stop. Stanley listened but wished the guy would shut up.

Work on the deck continued throughout the summer. The job became a Morgan family affair when Stanley's two sons joined his work force. Twenty-two and twenty-four years old, they brought strong young bodies to the task. Work now progressed rapidly. Often Brenda ran errands and asked the work crew to watch her kids after school. One afternoon, a neighbor from directly across the creek saw one of the Morgan boys leaning on the deck, his back to the wood. Brenda faced him in a posture of intimacy, their bodies nearly touching. The boy braced himself against the railing with hands behind him.

Stanley was anxious to complete the job. Brenda's flirtation with his sons was an obvious deterrent to their progress. Her friend, Jim's visits became more frequent. The guy's arrogance irritated him. Stanley didn't pretend to be a psychoanalyst, but Jim's conceit tested his own self-control. Even if Jim had personal problems he didn't need to parade his self-importance so openly.

In early November, Stanley came to pick up his tools and settle finances with Brenda. His wife accompanied him, the first time she'd met his client. He breathed an inner sigh of relief when the meeting went successfully. He'd remain friends with Brenda but was happy the job was done. Too much stress.

CHAPTER TEN

New Friends, New Securities

When the deck work was finished and Stanley's *friendship* remaining exactly that, Brenda yearned for new challenges. She accepted that they would not be moving to a larger, more expensive house in the near future. But she wanted *hers* to be freshened and in good shape in case the opportunity to sell arose. The house was plenty big enough for the family. However, new homes in the Deer Creek area appealed for additional reasons. Subdivisions there offered granite countertops, office-space rooms, increased storage, bathroom spas and pantries. Developments north of Lansbrook also were miles closer to North Pointe Baptist Church.

Both Brenda and Rob spent more hours at the church. Rob and the children drove there during the week for Choir practices. A mid-week service and study time became routine. Rob was dedicated to an early morning Men's Bible Study group. Avid devotees, he and Ronnie Stump rarely missed a session. As newlyweds, both had been active participants in a Bible study at Village Baptist. Through the passing years their friendship had deepened.

Ron's security alarm business kept him busy. Like Rob, he worked long hours to develop new customers and keep former ones satisfied. The construction business was beginning to expand, climbing out of a recessionary period. Ronnie's personality was a good fit for Rob. With similar backgrounds, the two shared religious beliefs. Brenda accepted the comradeship and got along with Ronnie's wife as well. One evening, at a social event, Brenda asked her, "What's Ron's favorite hair color?"

When his wife told Ron about the unusual question, he let it pass. But he remembered Brenda's odd query when the four ate lunch together after Sunday services a short time later. Brenda's hair glistened in the sunlight, a distinct change from her nearly-ebony hue.

"Do you like my new style?"

Ronnie replied that he did. A rich auburn-red shade with copper highlights made a dramatic difference in her appearance. He wondered what color she would come up with next.

Brenda continued to befriend new members at the church. She was a gifted greeter and welcomed new member, James Pavatt, into their Sunday school class in the spring of 2001. James' wife, Sukhui, attended services at the South Korean church.

James told classmates that he'd served in Osan, South Korea while in the Air Force. Sukhui had owned a shoe store there when they met in 1991. They married in Seoul, on June 19, 1992.

James had told Sukhui that he'd been drafted into the Air Force at age nineteen.

"They drafted me because I was good at shooting. They needed me for jobs in the Special Forces," he had said.

He became disenchanted with the Special Forces work on the occasion when he'd accidentally killed a friend while they were on a mission. Soon he began to hate the work and wanted out. Shortly after the marriage, he and Sukhui moved back to the States, to Oklahoma City. Sukhui's sister and mother moved there in 1992.

James had a grown daughter, Janna, offspring of his first marriage. Divorced, she and her five-year old daughter lived in Oklahoma City. He was a softie for his granddaughter and wanted to spend more time with the family. Sukhui wasn't much older than Janna and felt uncomfortable with the daughter who could have been her sister. No outright antagonism breached the family relationship, but tension existed.

When they returned to Oklahoma, James had left the Air Force and had become an Insurance sales associate for Prudential Insurance Company. In the following years he built a clientele for his services. He continually prospected and saw his new church family as a natural avenue for his insurance sales.

Sukhui remained uncomfortable outside her South Korean church. James chose the Baptist congregation at North Pointe. He took Sukhui with him to North Pointe several times in order that she might meet his new found friends. He began to spend more time with them and less with her. Tension grew in their marriage. By spring, 2001, Sukhui felt more and more alone.

Brenda had welcomed James into the North Pointe congregation, where he became a good friend to her and Rob. He joined the little group that gathered for a meal or coffee after church events. One evening, James opened the discussion.

"You know, with Rob's increased traveling, you two might think about carrying more life insurance," he said.

"I have thought about that lately," Brenda replied.

"The risk factors definitely increase with his business travel. I'll look into some possibilities that will accommodate you. Brenda should have sufficient financial security for the future, as well as the children. Rob, they wouldn't have money worries if, God forbid, you'd suffer an untimely death."

Rob and Brenda agreed that James should pursue the research and locate the right policy for their needs. By late spring, he had come up with a plan for adequate coverage with Prudential.

It was clear that he did his homework. The policy would grant $800,000.00 to Brenda as prime beneficiary on Rob's demise. Upon her death, the contract provided for the kids. Otherwise, she'd be their trustee until they reached maturity. The agreement appeared acceptable to all and Rob signed the papers to activate the insurance. James had ensured them future financial protection.

Activities at the church consumed much of their time. While Rob continued with his men's group and choir, James and Brenda agreed to teach a youth Bible class together, from late spring and through the summer months. Brenda and James enthusiastically planned the curriculum for their sixth graders. Brenda wore short skirts, like the ones her students sported. She talked with the girls about the latest fashions.

By late in the summer, rumors circulated about the couple who taught the sixth-grade class. Tongues wagged. Not only did she look like one of the pre-teens in her class but her clothing was far outside the unwritten but accepted dress code for Southern Baptists. James and Brenda acted more like a dating couple than teachers. Furthermore, the teaching pair sat together in services, closer than married couples. Brenda's kids seemed comfortable with James but her husband was not. Rob's ears burned with the insinuations he heard muttered behind their backs.

On September 16, Rob played in a charity golf tournament and arrived late for the evening church service. He sat down at the end of a row with Ronnie. He passed a note down the aisle to Brenda, seated next to James. She read Rob's note and glared at him with contempt. After the service, they stacked chairs. Ronnie noticed the hostile look on Brenda's face. In the parking lot, Rob sat in his car with James leaning through the driver's side open window. Ronnie could see that Rob was excited and upset.

"You set me up!" James's face flushed while he shouted at Rob.

At this point, Ronnie intervened.

"Come on, Rob. Let's go to McDonald's," he said.

The two went to the fast food chain, had a drink and talked. Rob had heard from a former church minister.

"He saw Brenda having lunch with James. They looked too cozy to him and he told me. Did you know about it?"

"Yeah, but I didn't think anything about it. I assumed they were planning lessons," said Ronnie. "Maybe you should talk to the Board of Deacons if you think something is out of line."

Ronnie recalled a talk he'd had with Brenda a week earlier. He'd heard the rumors and wanted to protect his friend. They spoke after taking her kids back home from *his* house. The Andrew house was messy, hadn't been cleaned up in a while. Ronnie confronted her about the unusual relationship with James and the effect it was having on *his* friend.

"When was the last time you and Rob had sex?" he asked.

Her face flushed. Her eyes flashed contempt.

"That's none of your business. I hate him and I only stay with him for the money."

Ronnie thought back. On an earlier occasion, at Braums, she'd also confided her dissatisfaction with her marriage. She had blurted, "I hate him. I bought a lottery ticket and hoped that I'd win. If I won the lottery, then I could leave him."

The venom in her comments, and now the open relationship with James, disturbed Ronnie. He'd been wrong not to tell Rob about the accusations he'd heard in the church. He knew that Rob cared for Brenda and wanted their marriage to be above reproach. On the other hand, Brenda's actions pointed in the opposite direction.

On September 19, a group of church leaders, including Deacon Terry Allen called James and Brenda in for a meeting. Blunt, they asked the couple to stop teaching and to resign their membership in the congregation. When Ronnie heard the news, he went with the two to El Chico's Mexican Restaurant. He wanted to hear their story.

"I don't think it was the best way for them to handle this situation," he said.

"We've been kicked out of the church." Brenda was overcome with emotion. She cried openly. With equal gusto, James ranted his feelings.

"Have you told Rob?" Ronnie asked.

Brenda called Rob on his cell phone. The Wednesday night calm of church classes was shattered. She accused Rob of siding with church officials in her embarrassment.

James was nearly out of control. "I hate the son of a bitch!" He shouted.

"I think you should back out of the relationship," said Ronnie. It's not too late for you and Sukhui to patch things up. She's a nice girl and doesn't deserve to be cast aside. Brenda's a married woman with two kids and a husband."

At this point in time, Ronnie's sympathy was entirely with his best friend. Rob called him to ask a favor.

"James cussed me out after church," he said. "Seems he's blaming me for the trouble with the Elders. Do you have an extra bed? I may need a place to stay tonight."

Rob deserved a loving wife who would be faithful to him. He'd been stoic in his faith in Brenda. Ronnie knew that he had written sentiments of his hopes for her to return to him with love in her heart. Ronnie hoped that Rob's deepest wishes would come true.

CHAPTER ELEVEN

Hot Tub Friends

For us, the summer of 2001 promised to be busy. We left Oklahoma's blast-furnace heat and moved into our "home away from home" in Colorado. Three months in the mountains was a welcome change.

Before we left for Colorado, I congratulated Brenda on her early Father's Day gift for Rob, a top-of-the line hot tub. She had it delivered and placed on the concrete patio outside her kitchen door. It was serviced and filled for their enjoyment in the hot, sticky days ahead. Connor had allergies and asthma. She hoped the steam would open his clogged nasal passages and gave him relief from the seasonal misery.

One Saturday in early June, Dean was mowing our lawn. Standing at the kitchen sink, I heard a robust splash outside and glanced up. Rob had climbed in the hot tub for a yard work break.

He shouted to Dean. "Why don't you all join us? The water's great."

I hesitated. We needed to pack for Colorado, but Brenda echoed Rob's invitation. We gave in and changed into swim suits. In a matter of minutes we sank into the bubbling water.

Rob's enthusiasm for the hot tub was contagious. "What do you think of my Father's Day gift? Brenda made a great buy."

Before either of us could reply, Brenda offered. "Oh, it's for Connor's allergies."

Dean teased her. "Brenda, Rob's going to want to see you in a bikini in here,"

But Brenda shook her head. "No, the kids will use it more than we will."

After a dunk in the gurgling oasis, we joined them for a drink and a toast to the new purchase. Despite the fact that we were closer in age to their parents, that day I felt a kinship with them.

I gave Brenda our summer address, telephone number and particulars about our son, Jeff, who would look in on the house and take care of the yard. She already had an extra front-door key, in case of an emergency. Less than a week later, we were en route to our mountain retreat.

In late June Brenda called me in Colorado. "We're having some friends over. Do you have a punch bowl I can borrow?"

"Sure." I was glad to help and told her where it was in the garage. Always a good neighbor, she would have offered me the same.

Over the years, she'd often been generous with a paper plate of cookies or pumpkin bread that she'd baked for a family or school occasion. I hoped her party would be a success.

— — — — — — — — —

Midsummer, 2001, was a relaxing one. We hiked the mountains, entertained family and friends and wished for the vacation never to end.

At home in Oklahoma, however, the Andrews were frustrated by a gigantic pipe leak flooding their master bathroom. Brenda called on a plumber, David Head, to solve the problem. He worked hard but the leak was persistent, with heavy damage to the carpet and flooring in the entire room. Brenda watched the expenses escalate each day. Furious at Head's lack of success, she fired him. His costs exceeded $1,000.00. He wanted his money and pressed her for it.

Over the phone, Brenda agreed to pay him for his initial house call. He would stop by to pick up the check. Sensing a possible confrontation, she planned for a back-up.

Her next door neighbor, a retiree, agreed to be with her in the front yard when Head arrived. In the meantime, Brenda changed her mind about paying him. She was not going to give him a dime. The doorbell rang but she denied him access inside the house.

Through the glass door, Head insisted she pay up. Brenda disagreed.

"I don't even have a receipt!" she screamed..

Disgusted, Head turned and walked to his van. She followed him.

"You mean this?" he said, picking up a yellow ticket from the front seat and waving it toward her.

Brenda grabbed the paper, ripped it in two and hurled insults at him. Head, barely inside the truck, now stepped back out, confronting her. For him, non-payment was not an option. He stood his ground when she yelled and waved the torn paper in his face. "I'll f . . . . in' kill you!" she screamed.

Head called her bluff, stepped into her face, their bodies nearly touching.

The neighbor, doing yard work by the driveway, interceded. He positioned himself between the two and faced the plumber.

"Don't be stupid," he told Head. "You can sue her, or whatever, but you'd better leave now."

"She cursed me out and threatened my life!"

The plumber turned away and climbed into his truck. He slammed the door, fired the ignition and peeled out of the driveway. He would not let the bitch get the best of him. Perhaps the old guy was right. He'd fight her for the money and win in court.

— — — — — — — — — — —

A slow process began, repairing the flooded Andrew bathroom. Brenda called us again.

"Hey, Judy," she said. "We've had a leak in the bathroom. Now the plumber wants to shut off water in the entire house. Do you mind if Rob brings the kids to your house for showers?"

"Of course not, use whatever you need," I answered. "You've got a key."

I thought nothing more about it, happy to be able to help in a crisis. Meanwhile, our vacation was nearing an end. After spending a weekend in Kansas to shorten the long drive, I was anxious to get home to see my little granddaughter. Dean, on the other hand, had planned a weeklong stay at the farm. He loved riding along in the combines when the crews harvested our corn. Brought back his "farm boy" memories, he said. But I was a city girl and drove back to jammed grocery aisles, traffic jams, leaves that needed a rake and the prospect of quiet in my house. Instead, on my first night home, something skittered across the carpet.

In typical response, I screamed when the little furry booger zipped behind the TV. I hated mice, but decided against calling Rob to come over when I glanced at the time. Tomorrow would be soon enough. I shuddered and ran upstairs to my bedroom where I would be safe from the impending hoard. I telephoned our son, Jeff. He suggested mouse traps. Men!

Early the following morning I knocked on the Andrews door, eager to relate my horror story. I wanted to know if Rob had noticed hostile critter activity elsewhere in our house when he'd used the bathrooms. Brenda opened the door and gave me a welcome hug.

"Did Rob notice any mice running around my house?" I blurted.

Brenda didn't answer my question. She seemed distracted and her lower lip quivered. She wanted to talk, but not about my rodent problem. She began to cry and tried to blink back the tears.

"Whatever on earth is the matter?" I asked.

She sighed and explained between halting breaths. "Rob and I are separating. He's moving out to an apartment. I don't know what to do."

In consolation, I hugged her while she told her story. "We've had troubles for years," she said. "Rob even moved out when we'd been married for ten years. He lived in his car that week. We got back together, though, and he moved back home."

"What *are* you going to do?"

That was the wrong thing to ask. Brenda's tears overflowed. I tried another comforting hug, but it did little good.

"I don't know," she said. "I don't want to have to go back to work."

"What brought all this on?" I really was curious because she and Rob had seemed so happy. A scant three months earlier, our date with them in the hot tub had been light and frivolous, certainly free from tension. I heard her story between sobs and halting breaths.

"It started when my friend, James and I were teaching the

class at church. People said my dresses were too short. Rob got jealous and turned the church people against us. They asked us to quit teaching, and to leave the church."

Her explanation ended with another crying outburst, a faucet that would not turn off.

Dumfounded, I could only mother her. My concern was genuine.

My mouse infestation was minimal compared to Brenda's crisis. Her children's stability could unravel with a divorce. I felt like crying with her, but tears solved little.

"I'll be here for you, for support." I said. "Whatever you need . . . ."

She dried her eyes and attempted a bleak smile. "Okay, I'll let you know," she said.

I returned home, deeply troubled by the news from next door.

The following Sunday afternoon, Dean drove up to unload his new Subaru wagon, a purchase from our mountain town. Puzzled, he noticed Rob carrying armloads of clothing and small household goods to a pickup truck, one Dean didn't recognize.

"Hey, Rob. What's going on? Are you moving out or something?" Dean laughed at his own joke.

I stood near the doorway, to greet my husband. Wide-eyed at what I heard, I shook my head 'no.' but Dean was oblivious to my warning.

Rob blinked, then dropped his load in the truck and sauntered toward Dean.

"As a matter of fact, yeah. Brenda and I are separating for a while. But I hope to move back here soon."

Dean's smile evaporated. Numbness replaced his light-hearted mood.

Rob continued. "I don't want a divorce. I hope that Brenda and I can work things out, so this will just be temporary." His voice was hopeful, not sour. The man was an eternal optimist.

———————————————————

In the coming days, James Pavatt's white truck was parked in Brenda's driveway a number of times. Their friendship had not abated, despite what she led me to think. Now, she fixated on

Rob's character. At the mailbox one day, she confided to Dean.

"I'm sure that Rob has a girl friend," she said. "It's that blonde, the one who works with him."

"Rob? He wants to make things right with you," Dean said. "Are you sure about something like that?"

Brenda was adamant. "Yes, I've got a friend looking into it. Rob's having an affair."

Dean shrugged and let it go. A hysterical female involved in a separation might jump to conclusions. He'd rather see a return to the hot tub days.

CHAPTER TWELVE

A Split in the Wind

I kept busy, getting my house back in order following our summer in Colorado. My thoughts wandered to the Andrews and their difficulties each time I went to the garage or to the mailbox. Now that Dean had retired, he was at home more than I. My days were filled with tennis, volunteering with Mobile Meals, shopping and family needs. We both stood ready to help Brenda, to listen while she sorted through her new possibilities. I found it difficult to understand her dilemma when seeing Pavatt's truck parked next door more often. His constant presence interfered with my supporting Brenda.

"My friend James is helping me," she explained on one occasion.

The school year began. Now Genesee and Connor rode the bus to school, mornings, and back home in the afternoons. In previous years Brenda had driven them to and from the school.

"Genesee's more independent this year. She's in fifth grade and is more grown up now," Brenda said.

Most mornings, Brenda stood with them until the school bus arrived. Within minutes of its departure, neighbors on the corner watched her climbing into the white truck that stopped at the same pickup point. Later, she would step from the same truck in time to greet her kids at the end of their school day. After a brief time at home, she'd drive them to after-school athletic activities or playtime with their friends.

"What's going on with you and Rob?" I asked one afternoon.

Brenda's lip puckered and her smile tuned to a frown.

"Rob's insisting that *I* file for a divorce. He says it'll look better if I file than if he does." Worry lines streaked her forehead. Short breaths punctuated her sentences. I felt truly sorry for her.

"Don't you have any hope for reconciliation? Rob left Dean with the impression that he didn't want a divorce," I said.

She was indignant.

"He messed up any chance of that when he sided with the people at the church. He's turned any friends I had there against me. Besides, I'm sure that he's having an affair anyway, probably doesn't want to make it right."

"Oh, Brenda, I'm so sorry. Are you *sure* of that? Rob always seemed to be loyal to you and the children."

At the same time I remembered when Brenda had jumped to conclusions, taken things into her own hands with the neighbors. She'd marched up to the corner when the Blakeleys had their massive motor home parked in the circle drive for more than a few days. It offended her, and she used her children as an excuse.

"Dwayne, it's against the covenants to park the RV in front like you've done. Besides, my kids can't walk up the street, or ride their bikes and have room to see around it. It's downright dangerous," she had ranted.

Her rage didn't do much for neighborhood accord. But secretly, the rest of us in the cul-de-sac were glad she'd approached him.

Now, when she talked about Rob's having an affair, she spit the words with firm conviction. At this point I didn't know what to think. When I told Dean about the odd conversation with Brenda, he rolled his eyes in disbelief.

"Remember, Judy, you're hearing one side of the story," he said.

Later that same week, Rob came to take his kids out for dinner. When he talked with Dean, in the yard, he was more confident about their reconciliation than Brenda had been.

"I hope this blows over soon," he told Dean. "I don't want a divorce. Brenda will take me back and things will settle down again. I don't think she wants a divorce, either."

His optimism puzzled both of us when, soon after, Brenda told us that she'd hired a lawyer.

"Greg McCracken was recommended to me. He's supposed to be a good divorce attorney. Rob's hired a lawyer of his own, somebody from Enid."

I was stunned. Surely the little family next door wouldn't go through with this. I wanted to shake sense into them both. The misunderstanding at North Pointe Baptist had certainly gotten out of hand. It was hard to believe Brenda's explanation of those events. What a mess!

In the next few weeks Brenda opened up to us with more than the usual small talk. One day, she appeared smug when she told me her latest news.

"Rob's been keeping a journal for a long time. I tore out the pages where he wrote about me."

"Brenda!" I was shocked she'd do such a thing. "Aren't those his personal papers?"

"He wrote about me. I have a right to them," she said.

She never ceased to amaze me. My experience with divorce was strictly from the sidelines, watching others endure the process. I had seen friends allow emotion rather than reason to twist their thinking.

Soon after, Brenda told us both about another action she'd taken against Rob.

"Today, I took $90,000.00 from our joint account and opened an account in another bank. Rob will never be able to find it," she said.

"Brenda!" Dean and I both did a double-take at this one. "What on earth are you thinking?" We felt that she had been overly aggressive in the money matter.

"In case Rob decides to fight about a settlement, then I'll have enough money to take care of me and the kids. I don't want to have to get a job. My kids need me at home."

We didn't see or hear much about Rob in the following weeks. We *did* see more of James's vehicle, parked two or three times a week in the driveway. I casually mentioned his being there so often to Brenda.

"Oh, he's helping me with paper work," she said.

One afternoon Dean talked with Brenda while I was out. She told him about a visit to Jordan Associates.

"Rob's turning the people at Jordan against me, too. Not just the church members."

"What do you mean?" Dean asked.

"I went to his office. I wanted to have it out with him about the affair he's having with a girl from there. He was in a meeting and wouldn't talk to me, asked me to leave."

She was indignant, now. Her voice grew louder; her hands vigorously illustrated the story.

"I grabbed the remote from the TV on his desk. I just wanted him to talk to me. They had the nerve to call the security guard. The guy made me leave. It was so embarrassing — but I took this."

Brenda held out the remote she'd taken, a trophy of the office incident. Bug-eyed, Dean didn't know what to say, staring at her hand.

Brenda started to cry. "I hate him, I hate him!"

At this point, we accepted that a breakup was imminent. As friends, we consoled Brenda in the following days. Her anger waffled between hating Rob and concern for her future. She was emphatic about not returning to the job market. Her lawyers, now involved, steered events closer to a courtroom confrontation.

Meanwhile, Rob came by to pick up his kids several times a week. It was important to him to maintain a close relationship with them, despite roadblocks Brenda threw in his path. He flashed his carefree grin to the neighbors, but his inner conflict must have been a river on the rampage.

CHAPTER THIRTEEN

Car Trouble

Brenda filed for divorce and retained her attorney, Greg McCracken, of the Miskovsky and McCracken Firm. Rob was hounded by McCracken's continuous requests for financial information. Frustrated, he recorded in his journal, "I just wish Brenda and I could get back together. I miss my kids."

On a Sunday in late September, Rob unloaded his clothes and few pieces of furniture at an apartment complex close to his office. He stuck firm to the notion that his move would be temporary, that Brenda would give up this divorce business and welcome him back. The one bedroom apartment did at least have a covered parking space a short distance from his door. The parking spot was a remote likeness of his former garage.

In following days, Rob's visiting co-workers agreed the place was a mess, hardly a welcome retreat for visiting children. From the office, friends Shannon Stone and Judi Brown offered to help. With ingenuity the two young colleagues turned to decorating. To cheer him, they shopped for colorful items that spoke "cozy."

Judi insisted, "Rob, Your apartment needs a *lived-in* look. Your kids need to be comfortable when they come over. Curtains, a few pictures, even a floor pillow or two will help."

Rob argued that the girls shouldn't waste their spare time on him. But they were more stubborn than he, making several trips to the apartment to give the place more appeal. Grateful, Rob bought them dinner. One evening Shannon was the last to leave. Rob walked her to her car, unaware that from the shadows someone watched them.

By October 26, Shannon and Judi had worked wonders at Rob's apartment. But mornings when he was alone with a newspaper and coffee, memories swept over him like a tsunami. Perhaps challenges at work would lift his heavy gloom. The trip to his office was shorter than before, but today even his car, a sleek black '98 Nissan Maxima, reminded him of Brenda.

Since becoming a stay-at-home mother, she had made the major household purchases, especially cars. The truth was that Rob disliked the messy work, like negotiating a purchase price with a slick car salesman. Brenda delighted in the sales routine; she was good at it, and he was glad to be rid of the hassle.

When his previous company car's mileage and repair bills got out of hand, Brenda had bought the Nissan. Soon after, she purchased her first *Mom- mobile*, a dark red Chrysler Mini-Van. Roomy and loaded with extras, the leather interior pleased her, perfect for hauling kids and dogs.

Now, Rob's journal entries were full of anguish. His was not only frustrated over his failed marriage, but surprised at Brenda's hostility toward him. She resented his time alone with the children.

"I think she's a bit unstable," he told Ron Stump. "She's angry when I pick them up, stays angry at me."

On that October morning, Rob backed the Nissan out of his numbered parking space. He turned the wheel and eased forward onto the driveway. Rush hour. The thoroughfare was heavy with traffic. At the intersection, his foot dipped into an abyss. Where were the brakes?

On his cell phone, shaken, Rob called the service department at Bob Howard Nissan, got Phil Rogers, the service manager. Seven-fifteen.

" I — I pulled out," Rob told him. " Slowed down to make the turn and my brakes went all the way to the floor. I checked back in the parking space; saw a puddle of fluid on the pavement. The car's a '98. Thirty-four thousand miles on it. Don't you — think that's strange?"

"I'll send a tow truck out to pick it up," Phil told him. 'What's the address?"

Rob was emphatic. "No! I don't want *anyone* touching my car but me! I'll — get it there myself."

Between 9:00 and 9:15 that morning Rob inched the black Nissan into the service entrance. His emergency lights blinked on and off like an ambulance, taillights flashing a warning. For the early hour, the garage was busy. When he checked the car in, Rob talked to Phil for a few minutes, glancing over his shoulder the entire time.

"I'd like to talk in your office," Rob said.

He looked frazzled, kept scratching his head. Rob fidgeted, nervous, not the usual jokester Phil was accustomed to seeing for routine service visits. They went into the office and Phil shut the door.

"I think somebody's out to take my life," Rob said.

Phil needed his best customer relations face for this one. Rob was clearly panicked over the failed brakes.

"I'll get my guys on it right away and call you with what we find," Phil told him. "We'll call Enterprise and get a rental for you to drive while your car is in the shop. Wait here. They'll send a car to pick you up."

Shortly, a white Enterprise van pulled up in front of Phil's office. When the driver opened the double doors, Phil watched Rob step into the van and sprawl flat on the floor. The service van pulled out with no visible sign of its passenger. His conversation with Rob bothered Phil. And now this even stranger behavior. It was clear that his client was not putting on an act. Rob was scared.

Phil would have his technicians thoroughly examine the Nissan. He signaled them to get it up on the lift right away. This job was not routine.

— — — — — — —

Later that morning, twenty-five miles away in Norman, Oklahoma, Janna Larson answered her phone at Bank One. James Pavatt was on the line.

"I need you to call Rob Andrew at his office for me. Tell him that Brenda is freaking out at Norman Regional Hospital. They're going to admit her. He'll need to get there as soon as he can because the kids are with her."

"Why don't you call him yourself?" Janna replied. "I'm kind of busy here right now."

"I'm having an affair with the man's wife. I can't call him. Oh — *and* you'd better use a pay phone."

It sounded to her like a valid request. She excused herself for a morning break, left the building and walked to the pay phone at a nearby gas station. This scenario felt wrong. Felt like a teeny-bopper pulling a prank on friends. She dialed Rob's office number. When there was no answer, she left a voice message for him but declined to identify herself.

No sooner had she gotten back to her office when her phone rang again. Her dad sounded tense.

"How did it go?" he asked. His normally quiet voice had an edge.

"I left a message on the answering machine. He wasn't at his desk."

"You'd better call again. Here's his cell number. He needs to get down there. She's freaking out."

Janna was reluctant. But she understood the situation her dad was in. She'd make a second call.

Rob answered his phone.

"You need to pick up your wife at the Norman Regional Hospital," Janna told him. "She's there with the kids and is going to be admitted."

Janna vowed to stay out of her father's romantic business from then on. She felt like a squirrel teetering on the outermost limb, far from its nest. Not long before, Dad had convinced her that Brenda was a nut case.

"Rob is mean to her and the kids. He's abusive to them. Brenda's afraid for them to visit his apartment. She even asked me to kill him, or have Dan or someone else do it. Nutty?"

At the time Janna had been too shocked to respond. Clearly, Brenda was overreacting to her separation. For now, Janna had made the phone calls. It was time to go back to work.

Several hours later, near closing time, she glanced through the reflecting glass in the lobby and was surprised to see Brenda Andrew.

When Janna approached her to say hello, Brenda smiled. "I came to check on the balance in my account."

The woman looked okay to Janna, no freaked-out crazy person here. Despite Janna's earlier inconvenience, she was glad to see Brenda. The hospital visit must have been a false alarm. Could be Rob had calmed her down.

That evening, Janna dialed her dad at his apartment. In the background, she could hear Brenda talking on another phone.

Her father said, "Don't tell anyone about the calls you made today. Brenda's upset. Rob told the police about being called to go to Norman. He's implied that someone is trying to kill him."

"Dad, I saw Brenda at the bank this afternoon. She looked normal to me," said Janna.

Before they hung up, Janna heard Brenda shout at the person she had on her phone, cursing, out of control. Janna heard the words, "Brake lines? . . . .cut . . . .?"

She cooperated with her dad. She didn't want to ripple the waters in his romantic liaison as she had with Sukhui, his second wife. Brenda made Dad happy. He talked of marrying her, having babies with her. Janna hated to see him in the middle of a messy divorce. For his sake, she wished for a quick settlement in the Andrew case.

— — — — — — — —

Rob drove the loaner car back to his office and left the Nissan in the hands of the technicians at Bob Howard. Still frantic after the early morning shock of having no brakes, he couldn't concentrate on work. He jumped when the phone rang. It was Phil, at Bob Howard.

"Robert, your brake lines have been tampered with."

"I'll be right out. Don't do anything with them," said Rob.

Within thirty minutes Rob drove into the service department. Phil showed him where the front brake line had been severed.

"Looks like a clean slice, with a very sharp object, like a box cutter," observed Phil.

"Does that explain why I saw fluid leaking in my driveway?"

"Yes. Do you want to sign a work order for repair?"

Rob's panic showed. "I think we should call the police, don't you?"

He composed himself and made the call. "Officer, my brake

lines have been sabotaged," he said. The complaint made, he turned the phone over to Phil for the details. Phil described the condition of the lines, with the one to the left wheel cut more severely than the right.

"An officer will come out and take pictures of the car – where the lines were cut, and the cut pieces," he told Rob.

Rob demanded, "I want all the parts you take from the car saved and turned over to the police."

— — — — — — — — — — — —

Ron Stump answered his cell phone on October 26. Caller I.D. identified Rob. Ron picked right up. He'd been a willing shoulder for Rob's burdens through the entire separation. Each day had brought a new twist.

"Hey, buddy. I'm at Bob Howard Service Center and — my brake lines have been cut. I have to meet Brenda at Wiley Post later for a parent-teacher conference. Guess I'll have to drive a loner. Just letting you know the latest."

"Whoa, Buddy. Slow down." Ron's reaction was a slow whistle. "What do you mean – brakes cut? Are you sure about the car? When did it happen?"

"About an hour ago I was headed to work. They wouldn't...grab! I couldn't stop at the corner."

Ron took in a deep breath. He remembered the evening in September, outside the skating rink where Connor'd had a birthday party. Rob had confided in him about James Pavatt, Brenda's newest 'friend.' Ron remembered talking with Jim at church, the guy boasting about his top-secret military service.

That evening, outside the ice rink, Rob had told him, "I'm afraid she's found someone to kill me."

"Who?"

"Jim Pavatt."

Now, Ron thought his friend might actually be right. A few hours later Rob called him again, this time from the office.

"I got a call from a woman. She asked me to get to Norman – to the hospital there because Brenda is freaking out. She's got the kids with her. Guess I'll drive the rental car down there."

"Robert, I don't think that's such a good idea."

"I don't have much choice, if the kids are with her. I'll be all right."

Ron detected Rob's hesitation. He could tell the man was not himself.

"Call me when you get back. Let me know the deal, and if the kids are okay," he said.

"Sure. Later . . . ."

Again, Rob telephoned in mid-afternoon. Frustration edged his tone.

"Ron, she wasn't at the hospital and she didn't show up at the school conference."

"Sounds mighty strange, my man," Ron said...

"If my brake lines were cut, I could have been killed driving down to Norman. I tell you, they're out to get me."

"Why don't you go up to Enid, to your folks' 'til this thing cools down a bit? Get away for the weekend. Do you good to get away."

Ronnie's words were light but fear overwhelmed him. Rob had had more than a "bad day." The danger to his life was real.

The next morning, Rob told Ron that he'd talked to Brenda the past evening. She'd said she'd heard about Rob's brake lines.

"I don't know how she could have known," he said. "I didn't tell anyone *she* would have seen."

When they talked later that night, Rob appeared dumfounded by the events of the day, musing aloud, "Brenda really shouldn't kill the goose..."

The following day, Ron was relieved when he learned that Rob had, indeed, gone to Enid for the weekend.

CHAPTER FOURTEEN

Day for Decisions

"Rob wants me to file for the divorce." Brenda caught my attention at the mailbox one morning. "He says that if I file first, it will be easier for the children, and my reputation. He doesn't want to do it, I guess."

Dean had learned from Rob about the split and had told me. I figured *she* was the one who wanted a divorce. When Rob had piled his clothes and personal items into his brother's truck in late September, he'd been unhappy about their fighting. He'd seemed resigned to the move to an apartment, but emphatic about it as "only temporary."

Brenda's divorce attorney, Greg McCracken was a partner at Miskovsky and McCracken, a downtown Oklahoma City law firm with an impressive resume. The firm had a reputation for litigious settlements and was tenacious in a divorce court. McCracken docketed the preliminary hearing for November 1, 2001. He requested stacks of information from both Rob and Brenda. She gathered insurance forms, checking and savings account statements, tax forms and Rob's pay stubs, a voluminous paper trail for her future financial stability. A portion of Rob's income would be more than substantial to keep her and the children comfortable. Brenda was honest about her wish list. Insistent on two points, she wanted to remain a stay-at-home mother without having to sell the house. She was open about her "wants" when she updated us on her legal progress.

Rob, on the other hand, felt like a rudderless ship. The legal requests stung. In his daily journal, pages were full of his wishes for reconciliation with Brenda. Ron Stump was his confidant.

In public, Rob's pasted-on smile masked the uncertainty he felt. He dreaded the court date. In support, his father and Ronnie would be present.

During the week prior to the hearing, Brenda asked me for advice on her courtroom appearance. Another neighbor advised that she wear a dark or muted suit or dress, nothing bright or gaudy. She passed on his suggestion to me.

"I suppose that's right," she said. "When the people from church turned against me, they said my skirts were too short."

"A conservative appearance," I told her. "Wear perhaps a grey or taupe outfit. Think of what you wore when you worked at the bank, more of a business look."

"What about jewelry?" she asked.

"I wouldn't flash any big rocks or heavy necklaces. I have a simple gold cross on a gold chain, with a single diamond inset. You can borrow it if you like."

"Thank you so much," she replied. "I'll take good care of the necklace."

By the end of our conversation, her eyes had begun to water. On the other hand, my own spirits were high. My fashion advice had been an obvious hit.

"I have another favor to ask," she said. "My lawyer says I should have character witnesses in case we go before the judge. My friends, Stanley and Rick and another friend, Theresa will do it. I've asked Bee Jay and Pauline. Will you be a witness?"

"Sure," I said. I didn't hesitate, remembering how kind Brenda had been through the years, sharing baked goods and checking mail and papers. I wanted to help her out.

When the day arrived, I asked her if she needed a ride. She declined.

"My friend, Stanley, will drive me downtown. We'll meet at my lawyer's office. It's across the street from the courthouse, in the big glass building."

I established the time and address and offered to take Bee Jay and Pauline Garrison with me. Both were fifteen years older than I, and they appreciated the ride. On the way, we chatted about the Andrews' situation. Eager to support Brenda, we agreed that the children would be better off with her, with substantial alimony and child support. We'd all hate to lose our good neighbor. We talked about what questions we might be asked, and how much detail would be required. Rob's cut brake lines would not be *our* issue. We were neighbors, not close personal friends.

As an adult, I'd been in a handful of law offices. My legal experience included the purchase of a trust agreement and the reading of a relative's will.

McCracken's office in the Oklahoma Tower Building was spacious. His windows rendered a clear view across downtown. He ushered us into comfortable chairs around a large conference table. I fully expected to see a scrapbook chronicling the Andrews' history of courtship, marriage and decline.

McCracken was cordial. He shook our hands and outlined the procedure that would be followed once we arrived in the courthouse. He was a smooth version of my notion of a divorce attorney. In his mid-forties, his thick, black hair was tinged with grey, and he was of average height. He presented himself as his client's advocate; his intent was to fill Brenda's wish list.

It was a short walk to the courthouse. Inside, McCracken led us past a shoeshine stand and down a hall into a dingy coffee shop. Six of us made a tight fit in the straight-backed wooden booth where we'd wait. The smell of old coffee drifted from the small kitchenette.

McCracken said, "You know, we may not need your testimony. Brenda and I will meet with Robert and his attorney in a conference room at the end of the hall. She'll come down from time to time with updates on our progress."

I could see Rob and his father, Ronnie Stump, and another man at the opposite end of the hallway. Rob looked our direction, smiled and waved. I returned a weak smile. Brenda and McCracken disappeared into the conference room set aside for their negotiations.

Theresa, as it turned out, had been Brenda's friend through their children's school associations. Together, they had done the Brownie and home room mother scenes. I had seen Theresa's car in the Andrew driveway on occasion, but not as often as Stanley's or James's. Rick Nunley was a hard one to figure out. He was reserved, but he did volunteer the information that, when still married, he and his wife had been close friends of the Andrews. They had moved to Lake Arcadia. I recalled that Brenda had drooled over their new house.

Despite her wishes, Rob had insisted that they remain in Lansbrook.

In the dusky coffee shop, the minutes crawled by. Then, Brenda came in, smiling.

"It's gong okay," she said. "Rob's going to pay the house payments, plus an alimony and child support. I'll get to keep the house. But there is one big thing he won't settle on. It's the insurance policy on him. It belongs to me! I'm the beneficiary."

"What's the big deal?" I asked. An insurance policy would come into play only with a death, not a divorce.

But Brenda was agitated over the impasse. She wrung her hands. "I own that policy. *He* doesn't. He won't budge on it."

When she left to rejoin her lawyer, the rest of us talked. Not one of us could understand why she was so upset. An insurance policy was simply "insurance against lifetime catastrophe."

Meanwhile, we'd frequently heard the elevator doors open and close. Prisoners' chains clanked on marble floors as they were escorted to courtrooms upstairs. Late in the day, I was relieved when Brenda offered the points of settlement. Money would never be a boulder in her path. Rob's offer to continue making house payments seemed generous beyond duty. Brenda could remain a stay-at-home mom.

It looked as if we would not have to testify. Two or three more times, Brenda updated us. Tearful, she continued her anxiety about the insurance policy. Puzzled, we reiterated our joint opinion that she was inflating its importance. Genesee and Connor would be beneficiaries in the event of Rob's death. But Brenda insisted it be *her*.

Her final update was a relief.

"We can't agree on the insurance policy, but everything else is okay. A monthly check and keeping the house are important. And, visitation is part of the deal. I'll *hate* it when the kids go to see him."

I tried to be positive. "Brenda, you'll welcome the weekends they spend away. You'll have time to yourself, without dance practices or soccer to worry about."

"I guess you're right," she said. "I'll get used to it."

But her face was a mixed landscape, resentment behind stoicism.

When their conference concluded, Rob followed Brenda into the coffee shop. He shook our hands and flashed us his signature grin.

"Thank you for coming," he said. "I appreciate that you each took the time."

When he left, we collectively expressed surprise at Rob's warmth. Even in the shadow of litigation, he was genuine. He had been true to himself; a Christian who accepted differences but rose above them. I was both amazed and baffled. Details of the divorce were to trickle down in coming weeks, before the final settlement would be reached.

"I'll have the final decree around the first of January," Brenda told us. "I wish it could be sooner."

Feeling sympathy for her was easy. Rob would have the kids for Thanksgiving, she for Christmas. For Brenda, the next twenty days would be an emotional rollercoaster. For Rob, Thanksgiving Day would be too late.

CHAPTER FIFTEEN

Sharing Children

Halloween came just days before the Andrew preliminary divorce hearing. Ghosts, ghouls and goblins rang our doorbell early in the evening, hoping for trick-or-treat goodies. Colorfully costumed, Genesee and Connor came for candy the same as in past years. Brenda accompanied them without Rob. I offered extra goodies from my bucket. The Andrew kids had nothing to do with their parents' problems. They left my doorstep with wide grins and heavy bags.

According to Brenda, the temporary agreement allowed Rob one mid-week visit and to have his kids on alternating weekends and holidays. Thanksgiving, the next holiday, would be hard for her.

"I just can't stand it when they go to visit him," she said more than once in the following weeks. "I know it's the plan, but he doesn't have a decent bed for them at night. No telling what he feeds them."

Overly excited, she obsessed about food, sleeping arrangements, homework and emotional welfare. I scolded her.

"Brenda," I told her, "Rob is still their father. Your settlement gives him the right to see them often. Besides, except for the few weekends he'll see them; you get the privilege of tucking them in bed and waking up with them. Your home is theirs."

In the several times we talked, she alternated between tears and anger. "It's just not fair," she said. "I miss them so much when they go to his apartment. I just hate it. And I hate him, too."

There was no consoling her. Her resentment was like a river flooding its banks, gathering momentum, out of control. These scenes dripped with drama. Brenda had been a twirler in high school, always front and center for important events. Now, her reaction to Rob's rights was driving her to a crisis point. Her needs took precedence over his. *Now* I wondered if they hadn't always.

I was puzzled by her impassioned and angry voice. But I had not been through a divorce and was obviously not able to share her present experience.

Dean reminded me that we heard only one side of the story and to withhold my judgment for now. "Rob might be angry, too. He's got to come up with a hefty sum of money for her each month, *and* pay the house mortgage as well," he said.

One afternoon in mid-November, I lifted groceries from my car and had turned toward the Andrew house when a racket got my attention. Repeated 'rat-a-tats' sounded like gunshots. Jim Pavatt stood on the upper rungs of a ladder that leaned against the Andrew house, working a staple gun along the trim and above doorways and windows. He meticulously attached strings of bright green holiday lights, taking directions from Brenda, who stood below. He'd give stiff competition to any professional lighting company.

"You're going to make the rest of us look sleazy," I said, walking toward them, admiring the work. I would not install my own few multi-colored strings until well into December.

"My friend James needs to make another trip to Wal-Mart for more lights," Brenda said. "I don't have enough to finish the deck and behind the house. Genesee and Connor have always wanted to put up lights, but Rob never would. Now, *I'm* going to celebrate Christmas."

I'm uncertain how many trips the poor man made to buy additional lights, but that night he was Brenda's slave labor. The next evening we were treated to a spectacular light show next door. When Brenda flipped a switch, evenly spaced, brilliant green globes lit up the dark night. James's work had been worth the effort.

In the weeks following Halloween, the Andrews settled into a routine of sorts. The joint custody agreement gave Rob the right to invite the children to his apartment one night during the week. On the other hand, Brenda fought the sharing arrangement. Again, we became her sounding board. She told me about a specific evening when both children had gone to his place. With Thanksgiving getting closer, Genesee was swamped with homework. Connor was content playing video games and watching TV. In the telling, Brenda was near hysteria.

"He called 911 on me," she blurted. "He told the operator that he had a problem with me, with visitation."

"What do you mean?" I was totally ignorant about the night.

"He told them that I wouldn't abide by the rules — wouldn't let Genesee talk to me. I went over to his apartment when Genesee called me. She was crying."

"Wow," I said. "Why was she so upset?"

My question went unanswered. Clearly stressed, Brenda continued.

"I just wanted to talk to her, but he wouldn't let me. Made me stand out in the hall. He finally let me talk to the 911 person. She asked me if they were in bed. I told her that I'd already called 911 and said I was on the way to his apartment. Genesee wanted to talk to me."

To say she was distraught was an understatement. I listened and became further confused. I guess divorce affects reason when children are involved.

"The operator made me give the phone to Rob," Brenda continued. "He must have confused them because one minute he said I could talk to Genesee, the next, he said no. He'd asked for the police to come when he first called 911. At first, he said I could talk to my daughter, then leave."

"What happened after that?"

"I stayed awhile, and then I left. But I didn't want to leave them with him. I was worried he was making me look bad to get custody in the divorce."

I wished I'd never asked. I was concerned about her violent attitude.

Reminders of Rob's visitation rights set the pot to boiling. Anguish covered her face. Before she finished the account, she had worked up to a good cry.

"What are you going to do when Rob has them for Thanksgiving?" I asked.

"That's another thing. He's planning to take them to Florida for the holiday, with his parents. But my lawyer will put a stop to that. I won't let him take them out of the state."

I didn't reply but thought she might have to change her mind in two or three months when the final divorce decree was put into effect. Brenda's fight for sole custody loomed, monumental. I'd heard that judges were careful to award joint visitation rights to a father. Exceptions were uncommon unless the dad was a total loser, especially if he honored his financial obligations.

Brenda would have nearly a week to ponder plans for the holiday. I brought up our trip for the holiday.

"By the way, will you be around to look after our house? We're going to Dean's brother's farm for Thanksgiving. We're leaving on the seventeenth. We'll need a week's worth of mail and papers taken in. If you can't, I'll ask another neighbor."

"Sure," she replied.

"Do you still have our key?"

"Yeah, we used it a couple of times last summer. Used the shower and borrowed a punchbowl."

"Oh, yeah," I said. "You called us in Colorado both times. Have a nice Thanksgiving. We'll pick up the mail and papers when we come home. Remember, *you* get the kids for Christmas."

CHAPTER SIXTEEN

Death and Family

I kept up a feverish pace, washing clothing, packing suitcases and preparing food for our Thanksgiving feast. It was a family tradition. We would spend the holiday weekend in northeast Kansas, at Dean's family farm. The farm was a natural gathering place for all of us, coming from Kansas City, Oklahoma City and Colorado since his mother's death. Our sons, Mark and Jeff, planned on arriving the day before Thanksgiving. We drove north early to ready the house for company. Dean's brother, a bachelor, was glad to have our help.

Meanwhile, at home, each time I drove into the cul-de-sac after my numerous pre-trip errands, I smiled at the holiday display next door. Lighted or not, the decoration reminded me of Christmas rather than Thanksgiving. I might well be tired of them by Christmas.

Brenda's parting words stayed with me.

"I can't stand to be away from my kids at all," she had said.

"What are your plans?" I asked.

"James is taking me out to dinner. But it's not fair that Rob gets the kids."

I tried to reason one more time. "Think of it as a great time to accomplish things you can't do when they're here."

We hugged and parted, but I had little faith in my ability to shift her thinking.

In Kansas, Dean and I cheered our team on during the Saturday football game. Afterwards, we drove back to the farm to focus on housecleaning. By Tuesday evening, November 20, I was exhausted. The telephone rang and woke me from a collapse on the couch. It was Sarah, Jeff's wife, in Oklahoma City.

"Judy," she said. My parents watched Fox News tonight and heard about a home invasion on Shaftsbury, at the Andrew's. Rob is dead."

I was shattered. In disbelief, I stammered. "Wha-a-a-t?"

"Jeff called Bee Jay Garrison across the street to see about checking on your house tonight. He says the street is blocked off by police cars. They're stringing yellow tape in front of the Andrew house."

As if I'd been asleep, my brain jumped awake. "What else did he say about the robbery?"

"Just that both Rob and Brenda were shot and he's dead. I guess Jeff will check your house on the way to work in the morning. We need Hannah's playpen from there for our trip."

The shock left me reeling. I needed to tell Dean. "We'll talk to you after the ten o'clock news," I said.

At ten o'clock, the news was sketchy. The media called the event a home invasion gone awry, with a homicide. Brenda told the police that two masked men had come into the garage and shot them both.

"They ran out into the greenbelt," Brenda had said.

The greenbelt was a common area, banked alongside a concrete path and creek flowing through the neighborhood

We were stunned. Brenda had been wounded in the upper arm. A patrolman escorted her to the hospital. Next-door neighbors took charge of the children, who were unhurt. When the robbery occurred, they were watching television, waiting for their dad. Rob's holiday had ended in tragedy.

Dean and I couldn't stop talking about it. "Shootings don't happen in quiet neighborhoods like Lansbrook," he said.

"I can't wait until morning for more details," I stated. "Suppose I ought to call Brenda as soon as I can to make sure she's okay."

We conjectured, commiserated and longed for information. Neither of us slept much that night.

The next morning, I could stand it no longer. I dialed the

Andrew's phone number. I was surprised when Brenda answered. I told her that we'd heard the news from our kids.

I couldn't stop the flood of questions. "Brenda, are you okay? I heard you got a flesh wound. What about the kids?"

"I got back here a while ago," she said. "We stayed at a friend's last night. Rob's dead. It was awful!"

"I've been so worried about you," I said. "Does your arm hurt?"

"It throbs a lot, but it's not too bad now. What am I going to do? The police just released the house to me. I guess I'll have to make arrangements when they let me have the...Rob's body."

Although separated by a telephone line, I could hear real anguish in her voice. More questions spilled out.

"Do you have any family coming? I wish I could be there."

Brenda replied, "My mother is on her way from Enid to help with the kids. I don't know what I'll do..."

"Call me if you want to talk," I offered. "We'll be coming home on Monday, after the family leaves."

Long distance added to my helplessness. We spent Thanksgiving Day in Kansas, but our family celebration had paled. Our hearts were in Oklahoma City.

Jeff had videotaped the news channel segments about Rob's murder. The replays were spellbinding. Our neighbors' driveway glared at us from the TV screen, once a familiar picture, but now surrealistic. An Oklahoma City Police spokeswoman stood next to the live oak behind the Andrew's mailbox. Newscasters waved microphones in the policewoman's face, probing for a scoop. The taping began on Tuesday night, continued daily and ended when Jeff left for Kansas on Friday. Reporters zeroed in on early events in the investigation. No clues surfaced about the men's identities or whereabouts. Now, cynicism crept into reports about the possible suspects. No trace had been left at the crime scene to help nail the criminals.

On Friday morning after Thanksgiving our phone rang. This time it was Brenda. She was an emotional wreck.

"Rob's funeral is going to be on Monday morning at 10:00 A.M., at Crossings Community church. Will you come back to be there?" she asked. "I don't have anybody on my side. Bill Andrew's making arrangements, and Rob's parents won't talk to me."

Sympathetic, but puzzled, I replied. "Of course, we'll come home early, on Sunday."

Brenda went on. "Rob turned most of our church friends against me during our divorce. I want somebody there for me. His parents think I had something to do with his death. On TV, they are saying terrible things about me..."

A flashpoint of the TV coverage haunted me. But I assured her that we'd be home in time for the funeral.

CHAPTER SEVENTEEN
Coming Home

During the trip back to Oklahoma, Brenda's situation filled me with both anguish and anticipation. I couldn't stop thinking about our phone conversation on Friday. She had disrupted my thinking when she had suggested a rift with Rob's family, a greater separation than the divorce might warrant.

We pulled into our driveway late Sunday afternoon. I glanced at the Andrew house. A dull red minivan, the same model as Brenda's, but a more muted shade, occupied half her driveway. A light shone from the dining room window in the front of the house. First thing, we'd collect our mail. I hoped it was intact. I decided to telephone rather than to bother her this late in the day.

No one answered the phone. Perhaps she had left a light on when she had gone out. We'd deal with the mail and papers later.

Tired from the long drive, we dropped suitcases in our front hallway. The job of dragging them up the staircase seemed monumental. We decided to catch the TV newscast first. After the ten o'clock news, we lugged our belongings to the second floor. Dean tossed his clothes on the bed.

"Hey, Judy," he said. "Look at the bed. It's crooked."

"Oh," I replied. I was too tired to notice a bed out of kilter.

But he was right. Our wooden headboard sagged, one side off its two-inch support blocks.

He called, "Can you help me lift it back in place?"

I drew a breath and lifted the bed while he replaced the blocks. Then I looked across the top of the quilt and thought the patio door curtain looked strange. The hem was flipped up, as if a heel had caught in it. I didn't remember catching my shoe. Still, anything was possible when packing in a hurry.

With the bed straightening finished, I opened my suitcase and began tossing dirty laundry in a pile on the floor. I'd hang my clean clothes in the closet tonight, but the rest could wait until tomorrow. I grabbed a handful of blouses and opened my closet door. The space didn't feel right.

The small walk-in closet had grown more spacious in less than a week. My particleboard shoe rack had disappeared. The first instinct was to suspect my granddaughter. I thought about calling Jeff despite the late hour.

When he answered, I apologized. "Did Hannah play in my closet last week when you came over? I can't find the shoe rack from the floor of my closet."

"No, I went there alone to pick up the playpen in the other bedroom. That's all," he replied.

"Okay, thanks, and sorry to bother you."

I was puzzled. When Dean unpacked, his foot nudged something sticking out from under his side of the bed. Pay dirt. The shoe rack was broken into a half-dozen pieces, shoved under the bed. The broken rack hadn't walked itself into hiding. Something or someone heavy had fractured the shelf. Now I was afraid of my own closet.

Dean brushed past me into the closet space.

"Get me a flashlight and stepstool, please," he said. "I'm going to check the attic crawlspace."

When he climbed close to the ceiling, Dean spotted a narrow unpainted section of wood above the closet floor. The plywood covering had been moved, revealing a raw unpainted strip.

When I called Jeff again, I told him about the broken shoe rack and the possible intrusion in my closet.

"You'd better check the rest of the house," he said. "Call me back if you find anything else."

I felt like a character in a mystery novel. But this was real.

Now, uneasy in our own house, we began the inspection. We moved into the three remaining bedrooms. In the office, the corner bedroom overlooking the backyard and in the bathroom, noting was out of place. But in Mark's bedroom, the one overlooking the Andrew's deck and house we fund a surprise. A spent shotgun shell sat against the open closet door. It rested upright, the red shell casing rising upward from its brass base. It appeared as if it might have been placed there as a door stop. Our suspicions mounted. I placed a third call to Jeff.

"When you were here on Wednesday, did you see anything unusual?" I asked.

"No," he replied. "When I came in that day on the way to work, I checked the phone messages on your answering machine first. I got bored listening because all the messages were asking about the murder. I walked across the hall to Mark's room for the playpen."

"Was the closet door in that room open?" Dean asked.

"No, it was shut. An open door would have jumped out at me. The playpen was at the front of the pullout bed. Folded it down and stuffed it into the case. I didn't want to be late for work. Dad, you need to call the police."

I was listening on the extension and couldn't help gasping when the reality hit me. If someone with a loaded shotgun had been hidden in the closet, he might have shot my son. I fumbled for the business card left in our door by one Detective Hatfield. I understood he had called on neighbors earlier in the week.

Dean dialed Hatfield's number and requested his extension. After numerous rings there still was no answer. No answering machine squawked at him to record his message. Frustrated, he hung up.

I looked up the telephone number for the police station and a dispatcher answered Dean's call. He told her about the disturbed items in our house.

"We can send out a patrol car to investigate. Sir and give you a case number," she offered.

"Thanks, but it's late. I'll call a detective in the morning."

At 8:30 the next morning Dean phoned Detective Hatfield. He was asked again for the now familiar case number. What was it going to take to get help? Dean repeated his story from the previous night.

"My house is next door to the one on Shaftsbury where a crime occurred several days ago. When we came home from an out of town trip, I found a spent shotgun shell in one of our bedrooms. It isn't mine. The next door neighbor had a key to our house."

"Why don't you call the police number and have them make a report," the detective said.

Dean was shocked at his lack of interest. He gave Hatfield our number before hanging up.

A few minutes later, our phone rang. It was Detective Hatfield and his tone was urgent.

"Mr. Gigstad, the police should have secured your house last night. Have you moved anything?"

"No, we left everything the way we found it."

"We'll come right out," Hatfield said.

"I'm sorry, but we're leaving soon for our neighbor's funeral. We'll be home about noon or later."

"Fine, sir. We'll have investigators out by early afternoon."

When he hung up, Dean turned to me. "Hatfield must have shuffled some papers and realized I wasn't a kook. Still, it's puzzling he didn't show more interest the first time we talked."

Shortly after, we left for the funeral. We planned to meet Sarah and Jeff at the church. As we drove off, a glance at the Andrew house unsettled me. Brenda had probably gone to the church much earlier, but I half-expected to see her in the driveway. Now, it seemed odd that we would be paying last respects to her husband.

CHAPTER 18

Laid to Rest

On Monday, November 26, the air was crisp and cool, but sunlight warmed an otherwise somber memorial service for Robert Andrew. Friends, neighbors, employees, church members and family assembled quietly in the gathering hall of Crossings Community Church, in northwest Oklahoma City. The congregation swelled as people filed in from a crowded parking lot. North Pointe Baptist Church could not accommodate the large crowd that had come to pay homage to Rob's memory. We walked to our seats and waited quietly for the 10:00 A.M. service to begin.

The Reverend Wade Burleson, from Rob's home church in Enid, Oklahoma, officiated. Shortly after 10:00, he stood behind the pulpit and announced that the service would be delayed fifteen minutes because some family members had not yet arrived. Throughout the sanctuary, whispers were polite. Most knew that both Rob's and Brenda's relatives had more than an hour's drive from Enid. Finally, organ music signaled the beginning of the service.

Those who eulogized Rob's life spoke of his deep spiritual convictions. They emphasized his commitment to the Bible for guidance, mentioning his diary. The presiding minister, and childhood, personal and professional friends testified as to the depth of Rob's integrity. I wiped away a tear when I heard the last words Rob had entered in his journal, "...I have faith in God. I should walk with assurance of the things I hope for – a relationship with my kids, a loving wife, and a home that worships, laughs, and plays with love..." I glanced at the people sitting near us and saw that I was not alone in my reaction. Others fumbled for handkerchiefs as well.

On a lighter note, childhood friends from Enid remembered how Rob's incredible sense of humor, at times, got him into trouble with classmates and siblings. His fun-loving personality masked his lack of physical grace.

A friend from Jordan Associates described the former Vice-President as persistent, encouraging, and able to overcome most obstacles. Inspired by a childhood book, Rob believed the story, *Green Eggs and Ham*, by Dr. Seuss, to be about the ultimate salesman. He kept a copy in his desk drawer at the office.

Anecdotes from his childhood softened the grief. Enid family friends remembered those incidents of a capricious boy who matured into a creative, loving adult. Rob's love for his children was apparent in the words spoken that morning, as well as his hope for reconciliation with his wife. Additional journal entries reflected his dependence on God's help to face his marital problems. In all, the service was a memorial faithful to a life well lived, a tribute to Rob's belief in God.

Ushers guided family members from the worship center before the remaining guests exited. Rob's parents, three brothers with their wives and children, and extended family and close friends filed out. Brenda's family followed — Rose Evers, and Brenda's sister, Kim Bolin. But Brenda, Genesee and Connor were not there. From the beginning of the service, *they* had been the missing family members.

I heard the questions spreading among the crowd gathered in the vestibule. "Did you see Brenda? Or the kids?" We shook hands with Rob's parents but we'd not have the chance to console Brenda that morning.

Dean and I visited with several mourners but walked quickly to our car. We had an appointment to keep. When we arrived back in our cul-de-sac, a black-and-white patrol car blocked our driveway.

A policeman met us. "You'll have to wait outside the house until detectives and the crime scene unit arrives."

He told Brenda's mother, who had just driven into the Andrew driveway, the same thing. Dean's early morning call to Detective Hatfield must have generated concern at the police station.

Within a short time an unmarked car pulled up, followed by a white police van, carrying the crime scene investigative unit. Two plainclothes detectives extended their hands to Dean and introduced themselves as partners. Detectives Kirby and Whitehead were friendly, but businesslike.

They allowed Mrs. Evers into Brenda's house after a careful check of the building yielded no further suspicious activity. Rob's parents had contacted the police when Brenda and the children had not appeared at the funeral service. Her mother seemed concerned as well. The police found no evidence that they were in the residence, nor had they recently been there.

The detectives and crime lab unit personnel came into our home and questioned us. Dean showed them the evidence that he suspected proved entry inside. He forged ahead with a question.

"Why was I ignored when I first called about the things in my house being out of place?"

"Detective Hatfield is with the robbery and burglary division. He happened to be on call the night of the homicide, but that is not his usual beat. We were involved on another case," said Detective Kirby.

"Oh," said Dean.

In the next half-hour, he took the detectives through the rooms in our house that had been disturbed. When they entered the bedroom that overlooked the Andrew deck and saw the shotgun shell positioned in front of the open closet door, Detective Kirby asked, "Did you touch the shell, Mr. Gigstad?"

"No, I didn't. When I saw it I figured that it was tied in with the crime next door. Brenda Andrew had our house key, to take in mail and newspapers while we were gone."

They moved closer to the closet door. Photographs were taken and the shell was picked up by skilled, gloved hands. It was identified as a 16-guage shotgun casing.

"That's a rare type," Dean said. "What was the caliber used to shoot Rob?"

"A 16-guage shotgun."

Dean drew in a deep breath while he digested the news. Involuntarily, my hand flicked up and covered my mouth.

"What was Brenda shot with?"

"22-caliber."

Shock that the killer had been in our house overwhelmed me. My instinct after talking with Jeff last night was confirmed. Crime lab personnel went to work gathering evidence throughout our house and attic. When Dean saw the size of the policeman who climbed into our crawl space, he couldn't resist asking, "Have you ever gone through a ceiling from an attic?"

The man grinned. "Don't worry. The department has liability insurance."

The officer returned to closet, bedroom and attic areas, collecting additional evidence while the two detectives questioned us in the living room. When the lab team finished their search, they removed several bags of evidence. The broken shoe rack was among the items.

"What else did you find?" asked Dean.

"Some shells followed a path in the crawl space across the attic," said the young man who'd been up there for a long time. His face was flushed. Sweat beaded his brow. Despite cool autumn air, the attic was a hot box.

Now, my suppositions about the happenings on the night of November 20 became real. My son, Jeff, had been in danger the following morning. I was no longer comfortable in the house. The missing house key was nowhere to be found. Nor had our newspapers and mail been returned. It would be a good idea to call a locksmith.

Before Detectives Kirby and Whitehead left, they assured us that we'd be notified of progress in the case as soon as possible. I didn't doubt him, but I was surprised to receive a call only two days later.

"Mrs. Gigstad, I want to let you know that we have just issued warrants for the arrests of Brenda Andrew and James Pavatt. It'll be on public record in the morning."

When the news broke the next day, Shaftsbury became the subject of national media attention. Television trucks, minivans with cameras mounted atop them filled the street for days on end. An international manhunt was now underway.

CHAPTER 19

Winter Sets In

The week following Rob's murder brought a barrage of local media inundating the cul-de-sac residents with more business cards than weeds in the greenbelts. Well-meaning reporters wanted the facts from those of us who could give first-hand knowledge of the Andrew family. Most were respectful, but they all wanted a scoop. Not only had Brenda not attended Rob's funeral, but neither did she take the children to school on Monday, leaving more questions unanswered for the media.

Because our house had been invaded, Dean and I became objects of curiosity. We agreed with detectives not to divulge what evidence we'd found. When the doorbell was not chiming, the telephone was ringing. We joked about drawing straws to see which of us would answer next. In all, the reporters were pleasant and respectful. Cherokee Ballard, the TV 9 reporter, came to our door late one evening, after visiting her mother nearby. She showed genuine concern and was sympathetic to our feelings of having been betrayed.

During the next few weeks, it became a daily occurrence to watch cars slow at our corner, turn into the street and ease by all six houses. Curiosity is a powerful motivation. Those of us who saw the intruders coined not-so-nice phrases for them. We felt like Southeby's was holding an auction, and 6112 Shaftsbury was the *piece de resistance*. Potential bidders drove by, agape at the merchandise, made mental notes and exited. We occasionally called out to them, simply to embarrass. But curiosity-seekers are not easily intimidated.

When December came, I looked at the Andrew house and felt an acute emptiness. Genesee had been so happy before Thanksgiving because she'd been chosen from a class of junior ballerinas to dance in the Christmas season production of The Nutcracker Suite. The dancers selected were the envy of ballet students throughout the city. She had practiced long hours for the part. Brenda had styled her hair in the traditional ballerina's bun, driven her to workouts, tryouts and practice sessions for the ballet. Now, Genesee would not perform. The junior tap-dancer in me ached for Genesee's lost chance in the spotlight. E.R. and Lou Andrew attended a performance of The Nutcracker in honor of their missing granddaughter.

Closer to Christmas, the dark house next door was a sharp contrast to the festive lights that graced rooftops throughout Lansbrook. Brenda and James had worked hard to decorate her roofline and trees long before Thanksgiving. Perhaps Brenda had taken a jibe at Rob's sense of appropriate display timing. Now, the darkened house seemed a gloomy contrast. No happy family would celebrate Christmas joys inside it this season. When I strung my few twinkle lights in the bushes outside my door, my heart ached for the darkened house next door.

The police had more information. A week after Rob's murder, someone had attempted to use an ATM machine with a card belonging to a James D. Pavatt. No statement revealed whether the machine in Nuevo Laredo, Mexico, had yielded cash. The fact supported the idea that the runaways had entered Mexico, one of Brenda's favorite vacation spots. Their point of entry was at Laredo, Texas. Thousands cross there every day, making individual tracking nearly impossible, but the FBI worked with the Oklahoma City Police and issued an alert for the pair.

Much later, in early February, documents revealed that Brenda and James were issued tourist visas in Mexico on the same day that the bank credit card was used. The visas allowed travel for 180 days, destination Monterey, the coastal area and Mexico City. I conjured up a mental picture of Brenda and Genesee having their hair beaded on a Mexican beach. Arriving home from previous vacations, Genesee had kept her braids until the beads fell out.

According to police sources, James Pavatt had asked a witness to notarize a document to allow him to take the children out of the United States. Rob Andrew reportedly authored the document.

On December 1, Brenda's relatives told the police that she was fine and would be talking to authorities shortly. Now, the media focused on these same people who expressed concerns for Brenda's safety. Rose Evers and Kim Bowlin appeared in a TV interview saying they believed that Brenda and her children had been kidnapped. Brenda had told her family that she and the children would sleep in a hotel room the night before the funeral, to avoid the media. Her mother believed they were abducted from their hotel. At the service, Rose looked solemn in a dark dress, and supported by her sister-in-law, Marilyn Evers.

Greg McCracken said, "They don't have any idea where Brenda is. This is out of character for her."

The family criticized the police investigation. Kim said, "Remember, there are always two sides to every story."

In December, I received a call from Brenda's divorce attorney, Greg McCracken. He asked if I had heard from Brenda.

Flippantly, I replied, "I assume that you know where she is and have heard from her."

He was silent. He then asked, "What evidence did the police find in your house?"

"We've agreed not to disclose that information," I said.

Then he continued. "I have Rose Evers on the phone line. She's worried about Brenda and wants to know if you know where she is."

"I'm sorry, but I don't know a thing about her whereabouts. I hope she'll be found soon, and safe."

When I hung up, I steamed. Now, I felt used by both Brenda's attorney and her mother. I was sure McCracken or both of them knew where she was. Dean listened to my emotional outburst. McCracken would not learn what evidence was found in my house.

Along with first-degree murder, the FBI had issued charges of "illegal flight to avoid prosecution" against Brenda and James. At the end of November, the FBI offered a $15,000 reward for information leading to their whereabouts. Wherever they were, they were in deep trouble. At the time, my feelings were mixed about Rose and Kim. Using McCracken as their attorney, they had made a bid for guardianship of the children. As she had abused our friendship, Brenda may have betrayed them and their trust. The police spokesperson asked the family to cooperate with the FBI if they had evidence of abduction.

The Andrew family provided numerous media interviews. They hoped the children would be returned to Oklahoma. For the public's better understanding of the trauma Rob had endured during the divorce proceedings, they released portions of his journal. I watched the TV coverage with increasing sympathy for the Andrew clan. Bill, Tom and Tim reflected on the fears Rob had expressed, both for his life and the separation from his children. CBS's *Early Show* interviewed Rob's, parents along with his brothers at their home in Enid. Watching them, I tried to place myself in their situation. They had more guts than I possessed. In the interviews, the grandparents pled for the safety of their grandchildren.

Through the court system in Garfield County, E.R. and Lou filed for guardianship of Genesee and Connor. Countering, Rose Evers filed an objection to the Andrew's request. She asked a Garfield County judge to move the case to Oklahoma County, but Associate District Judge Richard Perry ruled that proceedings be held in Garfield County. At the same time Rose asked that her daughter's bank accounts and assets be opened, but her petition was denied also.

Police spokesperson, Jessica Cummins, frequently appeared on TV. She upheld her department's handling of the case. Brenda's initial willingness to cooperate with the investigation had not pegged her as a flight risk. Cummins said that the children were listed on the National Crime Information Database as missing and endangered. The information, linked to the warrants for Brenda and James, would alert authorities instantly if they were sighted. U.S. Customs Service officials had authorized worldwide distribution of the data. The U.S. Customs office was involved because of Pavatt's using allegedly forged papers to take the children out of the country. Wanted posters were distributed, describing the pair as "armed and dangerous." Genesee and Connor appeared on missing persons posters.

National emphasis on the case began to build. Along with CBS's The Early Show, CBS's *48 Hours*, syndicated *Inside Edition*,

ABC's *20/20* and Fox's *America's Most Wanted* contacted the Andrew family and the police.

With the tremendous media attention, my writing friends suggested that I should write a book about this string of bizarre events. At the time, I refused to consider it. I was still emotionally tied to the Andrew family. I couldn't share my feelings with the public.

Later in December, I drove home one day and beheld an apparition in the driveway next door. It was Rob's black Nissan. E.R. and Lou had brought it to the city for filming of a segment of *America's Most Wanted*. The photo crew set up in the street, their cameras zooming in on the Andrew house.

Rob's dad also wanted to have the building winterized in case there might be bad weather early in the season. A plumber checked the pipes, the hot tub, and turned off outside water. Without heat, the place lay empty. I offered E.R. help in any way I could. Enid was an hour north, but it might as well be ten thousand miles in event of a plumbing or heating disaster. The Andrews appeared strong after the ordeal of their son's murder.

Brenda's mother, sister and aunt, Marilyn Evers, reappeared on TV with the same conclusion: that Brenda was a victim, not a murderess. At the time, I thought the words were hollow. I had a difficult time digesting the idea of "victim." From my standpoint, the evidence from our house showed her in a far less favorable image.

In 2002, Christmas came and went. It was a blessed time for my family, with relatives visiting from Kansas and both sons home. Jeff's own family had grown with his son's birth in October. But the house next door remained a damper on our happiness. Not only did the exterior look bleak, but the inside was cold. I prayed that Rob was safe with his God.

After the holidays, an occasional reporter came to our door. Each had the same agenda, to discover and divulge additional information about the missing woman and her children. The Andrew family's privacy felt like a scrapbook whose pages were dashed in the wind, vandalized by the written word. I was torn between the desire to help and the tendency to hide my deep-felt wounds.

CHAPTER 20

Before Mexico and Beyond

The next two months offered no closure to the puzzling disappearance of Pavatt, Brenda and the children. The FBI continued plastering missing person's posters of the Andrew children in Texas towns near U.S.-Mexico border crossings. Sufficient coverage might jog a memory enough for someone to make a phone call. On December 21, 2001, the FBI issued a $15,000.00 reward for information leading to the whereabouts and arrest of Brenda and James. It appeared as if the fugitives had been swallowed into the Mexican population.

Behind the scenes, however, FBI authorities landed a windfall in the person of Janna Larson, Jim Pavatt's daughter. When the crime made the news, Larson began to piece part of the puzzle together and decided that she might be at risk for prosecution. Acting on the advice of her mother, an attorney, she contacted the FBI.

The day prior to the shootings, Jim had asked his daughter to switch cars with him. Not only had Janna's been the telephone voice telling Rob Andrew, back in October, to pick up his children at the Norman Regional Hospital because Brenda was to be admitted, but now she'd been used once more. That fall, Jim had been open with her about his intentions toward Brenda Andrew. He followed the woman like a lovesick teenager. Janna was blunt.

She asked him about a sexual relationship with Brenda. He'd been adamant in his reply.

"She's just been with him...her husband," he said.

Despite her father's words, Janna observed a more-than-casual friendship between the two of them. He and Brenda had offered to pick up Janna's daughter at daycare, becoming more involved in her life. On occasion, Genesee and Connor had accompanied them. Janna reported that Brenda talked negatively about her marriage. She told Janna that Rob was mean to her, abused her mentally. Privately, Jim backed up this statement.

In October, at Janna's house, his announcement had been clear. "Next summer," he said, "after her divorce, we're going to get married and have a child of our own."

Janna saw that events had become dramatic concerning Brenda Andrew. Jim told Janna that Rob called him about a life insurance policy that Brenda tried to change. Jim had tried to help her with the paperwork, but Rob got wind of the changes in beneficiary and was furious. He went over Jim's head, phoning his boss. When he found out, Jim thought his job may be at risk.

"Don't tell anyone about this," Jim had told his daughter.

Janna noted one more show-biz instance in the unfolding Andrew saga.

In November, Janna's mother had moved in with her and her daughter. Between them, car trouble was a common occurrence. On the 20th, Janna drove her mother's car to work. Jim called and offered to leave his truck in the parking lot for her. After work, however, the white Ford 150 wasn't parked where she expected it to be. She called him. It was odd, she said, that he didn't answer his voice mail.

The following day, Jim left her a message. Janna's car was still in the shop and Brenda had taken him to Lake Thunderbird the day before to go fishing.

By that time, Janna had heard about Rob's murder. She was thankful when her father returned her call from the previous day. Scared for them both, she blurted, "Did you have anything to do with Rob's murder?"

"Of course not," Jim replied. "I was drunk at the lake, fishing the whole night long."

The next week, after Jim and Brenda had disappeared, Janna

felt obligated to share her information with the FBI. There was more: on Friday, November 23, she met the two at the bank with the intent of adding Jim's name to Brenda's bank account. The transaction took only a short time. That day she watched her father's paranoia run rampant. Jim insisted that the police had tapped his phones because he was Brenda's friend.

Janna did not object when he asked yet another favor. She packed his computer, clean laundry and passport. After deleting recent e-mails from his long-time friend, Dan, she brought the belongings to Jim's attorney's home on Saturday night.

The FBI was interested. Their office had focused on the Andrew case when the two were declared fugitives. Janna was given a cell phone; her land line was tapped, making her an informant on her father's activities. Her phone rang several weeks later.

"We're being held hostage by Mexican bandits," Jim told his daughter. He sounded frantic. "We need $5,000.00 to be released. We need the money now."

FBI instructions prevented Janna from cooperating. Fifteen to twenty additional calls were pleas for money. Brenda had threatened to kill herself and her children rather than be executed by bandits. But Janna heard Genesee and Connor laughing in the background. She received FBI permission to wire $120.00 to Cancun, Mexico, instead of the most recently requested $1200.00.

The next call from the pair was angry, demanding the full $1200.00. On the phone, Brenda called Janna "a little bitch".

"I guess the wire transaction must have gotten messed up," Janna said. She didn't offer to send more.

By New Year's Day, 2002, Janna had wired $500.00, compliments of the FBI. Jim's angry voice scorched the lines when he phoned on January 18.

"I need $5000.00 immediately. If you don't send the money, I'll know something is fishy. You turn me in and I'll kill you, your daughter and your mother," he said.

Confronted with his ranting, Janna thought about the bizarre events occurring since she had met Brenda Andrew. Faith in her father's return to sound judgment kept her focused. She had heard him say once that he and Brenda planned to go to Argentina, where they would not face extradition to the United States. Mexico was convenient but not free from joint prosecution.

Connor later related that they had spent one night hiding in a boat they planned to steal. The aim was to sail it to Cuba, another haven from extradition. However, the vessel leaked, thwarting their scheme. The pair was exasperated by their lack of funds. They also must have been getting hungry.

— — — —

FBI sources kept a close eye on the retreat to Mexico. They would try to stop the fugitives' flight from that country to South America. Janna stayed in contact with her dad to lessen the risk. Pavatt's bank card had been used to obtain money in Nuevo Laredo on Nov. 29, 2001, a short time after tourist visas for the Andrew children allowed their admittance into Mexico. At the border, Pavatt had shown a letter allegedly signed and notarized by Robert Andrew, giving him permission to take them out of the United States. By the end of January, the trail seemed to grow cold.

Meanwhile, the Andrew grandparents had filed papers in Enid, in Garfield County District Court, for legal guardianship of their grandchildren, if and when they resurfaced. News programs rebroadcast pleas from both sides of the family for the safe return of Brenda, Jim and the children. Winter set in with a chill, turning the case into any icy stalemate.

Border crossing points, both in Mexico and the United States, contained computerized files of questionable personages from both countries. Hidalgo, Texas was one of the more active crossings, with more than 24,000 persons processed per day in 2001. Populated with over 5,500 and sitting on the banks of the Rio Grande River, Hidalgo was a convenient site for American tourists who planned to dine and shop in Reynosa, Tamaulipas. Likewise, Mexican citizens delighted in the popular Texas retail trade on the U.S. side. Daily traffic boomed at Hidalgo. Travelers there could view a twenty-foot long statue of a Killer African Bee, commemorating the site as the first confirmed location of the bees in 1990.

Along with the U.S. Customs Service and the Immigration and Naturalization Services, the Border Patrol and Texas National Guard united to ensure the safety and legality of all travelers. They conducted both initial and secondary inspections of drivers, passengers and vehicles. Primary inspection involved a quick passport review. More detailed inspections were held at border crossing lots when personnel thought it necessary.

On February 28, 2002, a white minivan drove from Mexico into the crossing zone. A white man was at the wheel. Inside were two children, a girl about twelve and a boy several years younger. The driver claimed to be the children's uncle, but his demeanor sparked a question. The girl was crying, and the boy seemed agitated. An astute crossing guard made a preliminary check of the occupants' identifications, and he detained them in the border parking lot, for a closer verification of their records.

A short time later, an automatic tag reader at the same crossing scanned the license plate of a 1992 Chevy Beretta carrying an adult male and an adult female. Noting that the license number had been placed on the lookout list by federal agencies, an agent pulled them over. The names, checked against a database, linked the two persons to arrest warrants issued by the FBI. The guardsman who searched their car discovered wallet pictures of Brenda Andrew with her children. The photos showed the identical children he'd seen detained a short time earlier.

By that time, Jim Bowlin, Brenda's brother-in-law, was answering questions in the Customs office. Kim Bowlin, Brenda's sister, waited in a motel room in McAllen, Texas, for her husband to return with the children. She would wait a long time.

Customs agents turned the children over to the FBI. By 9:30 P.M. that same night, their paternal grandparents, E.R. and Lou Andrew had arrived by private jet from Enid. Genesee and Connor were confused and upset but otherwise safe. Both appeared in good health. They flew back to Enid with their grandparents, to the loving care that they would provide.

The border patrol searched Pavatt's car a second time, revealing but a few possessions. Luggage, clothing, a few American coins, a few Mexican coins and five cans of tuna were scant evidence from a three month stay. Authorities reasoned that the pair returned in pursuit of their money at the Norman bank. Crumbs from fast food indicated a less than nutritious diet.

Oklahoma County District Attorney, Wes Lane, breathed relief. He was ecstatic over Brenda and James's detainment on the U.S. side of the border. Often, countries that do not carry the death penalty, such as Mexico, will not release suspects to authorities in countries that allow capital punishment. Waiving extradition from Hidalgo, Texas, to Oklahoma County, Brenda and James were anxious to go home...

Upon detention in Texas, Brenda telephoned her divorce attorney, Greg McCracken. He told reporters that Brenda was anxious to surrender to law enforcement officials when she was arrested in Texas. "She's certain to be exonerated of any charges," McCracken allowed.

In Oklahoma, however, police and county attorneys planned a different kind of welcoming party. Brenda and James, shackled, quiet and cooperative, rode from Hidalgo to Oklahoma in a 2000 Malibu van with bench seats, separated from its driver by caging and a Plexiglas window. Brenda sat behind Beverly Matthews, a Deputy Sheriff from the Oklahoma County Sheriff's office. James sat behind Brenda. They whispered at first, then relaxed and talked about their stay in Mexico; the beaches, mountains, friendly Mexican people and James as "being good to the children."

Later, I had a difficult time believing the rosy picture. The lack of money, the phone conversations to Janna, contents of the car and lack of visible food better represented the family's sojourn in Mexico. The reality muddied Brenda's vacation album.

The Andrews family in happier times.

The Andrew house. The garage of death ...

Back of Andrew house and deck.

Outside the Andrew's kitchen door.

Route to Gigstad house from the Andrew's kitchen and deck.

Shell found on floor and shotgun similar to that used in the crime.

Moving day on the block. The Andrew family leaves Lansbrook.

Left: Prosecutor G. Gieger.
Below left: Detective Damon.
Below right: Detective Garrett.

Above left: Janna Larson, a daughter wronged.

Above right: James Pavatt, lover or killer?

Right: Accident waiting to happen – Rob's cut brake line.

[Drawings by S. Mckay]

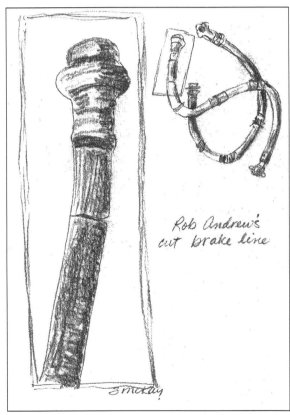

Rob Andrew's cut brake line

Red flags went up here when an astute border guard stopped the Pavatt/Andrew vehicle.

Brenda and James leave an Oklahoma County courtroom after a judge denied a request to move their trial out of the county. [Copyright 2003, OPUBCO Communications Group]

Maximum security unit, "A grey place."

Outside Women's prison in McLoud, OK.

CHAPTER 21

Legal Wrangling

When Brenda and James were detained in Texas, the legal hounds jumped into the middle of the story. Genesee and Connor became instant headlines, with each side of the family preparing to fight in court. Both the Evers and Andrew families held deep convictions that the children's guardianship should remain with them. Unable to participate in the legal squabble over her children, Brenda languished in the Oklahoma County Jail.

Upon their recovery, the Andrew children talked on the telephone with Rob's parents. E.R. and Lou Andrew were overjoyed. Lou was able to carry on a conversation with Genesee, but Connor was shaken and broke down crying. Before 11:00 the same evening, E.R. and Lou were passengers on a chartered plane bound for Texas, for a tearful yet joyful reunion. More than a month would pass before the children saw their mother.

Interviewed by media in Oklahoma City, Pastor Mark Sinor of North Pointe Baptist Church commented "...All are relieved for the safety of the children."

Robert Andrew's former co-workers were ecstatic over news of their recovery. A spokesperson for Jordan Associates stated that workers there were "thrilled beyond belief." Both groups voiced hope that the children would receive professional counseling.

The struggle over custody of the Andrew youngsters began before their feet touched the ground in Enid. Brenda's mother,

Rose Evers, had filed for custodial rights while the fugitives were in Mexico. Concerned for Brenda, she had joined forces with Kim Bolin, Brenda's sister, in the court battle.

But the Bolins faced a legal issue of their own. In early March, they were subpoenaed by an Oklahoma County Grand Jury. District Attorney, Wes Lane, sought answers to the Bolin's' questionable behavior at the time of Brenda's apprehension. His theory was that they may have assisted Andrew and Pavatt in their flight to Mexico.

On March 7, 2002, the couple was scheduled to begin testimony. Greg McCracken and George Miskovsky, Jr. represented the Bolins. But Assistant District Attorney, Fern Smith, moved that McCracken and Miskovsky be disqualified because they also represented Andrew in the criminal case. The two removed themselves and elected to act on Brenda's behalf.

Hearing the news, I was certain that the attorneys wanted the higher profile of defending a murder suspect.

The Grand Jury proceedings were recessed for a month, until April 9, 2002. At that time prosecutors would solicit testimony from Oklahoma City Detectives and FBI agents who were involved in the case.

The month dragged by. Legal maneuverings in Garfield County between both sides of the family made statewide news. Kim argued that her sister had the right to determine who should have guardianship of her children. As of Sunday, April 17, 2002 Genesee and Connor had visited their mother in the Oklahoma County Jail one time. Separated by a glass partition, they spoke to her on the telephone, with no physical contact. Both children were visibly upset and tearful during the encounter.

In argument, Kim contended that the children had not been allowed to see Brenda on Mother's Day in May.

Attorney Phil Outhier had been appointed advocate solely for the Andrew children's benefit. In Garfield County District Court, his opinion agreed with that of a teacher at their school. It was their feeling that the Genesee and Connor had improved emotionally but were still fragile. A stable environment would be important for continued progress. Outhier stated that he had received telephone threats because of his position.

By mid-June, E. R. and Lou Andrew were awarded the

children's temporary guardianship. Based on the future outcome of Brenda's trial, permanent custody would be decided by the judge. Kim vowed to continue her fight.

On a Sunday afternoon in April, my doorbell rang. Lou Andrew stood on the doorstep. She asked, "Do you still have a key to Rob's house?"

"No," I replied. "Is there something I can do for you?"

"I guess not. We made arrangements with Rose to meet here at the house. The children want their own beds, bicycles and a few other possessions out of the garage."

I offered my phone, but E.R. had already used a cell phone to call a locksmith. Rose had had the front door lock changed and today was nowhere to be seen. Ron Stump accompanied the Andrews in the cul-de-sac, offering help to E.R. and Rob's brothers. Genesee and Connor sat across the street in the Andrew's car. The locksmith arrived and reset the lock, and with no court order, the Andrews entered.

While I visited with Lou in the front yard, the Andrew men began to haul furniture from the garage. The work came to a halt when three black and white Oklahoma City patrol cars drove into our street and screeched to a stop in front of the house. One patrolman stated that a break-in had been reported. Dumfounded, E.R. answered the accusation with his explanation:

"Rose Evers has been issued a court order to deliver the children's belongings to us in Enid. However, we've had a hard time making contact with her. We decided to come here when we had help."

My eyes opened wide when I saw Rose Evers walk out of the house next door. She'd been inside the entire time. Meanwhile, her sister-in-law who lived a half-mile away in Ski Island drove up and parked in the driveway. The scene was becoming crowded. I could not shut my door without seeing the outcome.

Connor played in the front yard with Tom Andrew's toddler son while the adults talked with police officers. Genesee remained in Lou's car, tears streaming down her face. My heart went out to the siblings. Who could deny a child access to his bed or bike?

My better judgment did not prevail. While Rose voiced her feelings about the "break-in," I interjected. "Why can't you all talk it out and get along?" I asked.

Rose thrust a nasty look in my direction but did not answer.

By the time the vehicles had cleared the street, the property dispute was at a stalemate. Police suggested that E.R. contact the court before taking any belongings. I watched both Andrew children crying when the caravan drove away. Another bruise in their emotional suffering.

The disposition of the Andrew children's "stuff" would not be solved until later in June. At that time, a judge ordered the Evers family to deliver any remaining personal property to the children. In addition, Lou Andrew was to monitor supervised visits with the Evers.

My discomfort now became a weight. I had tried to overcome my feelings of being used by Brenda. Now, when I saw Rose's attitude toward her grandchildren, my sympathy for the Evers also underwent a change. I felt uprooted and tossed into the wind by a spring storm.

CHAPTER 22

Waiting in the OK Corral

The bitter pangs of winter weather had heightened the pain we felt following Brenda's flight to Mexico. Newspaper and video accounts of her capture provided the community relief about the condition of her children. Little information leaked into the streams of words printed about them, except for the overwhelming flood of thanks for their safe return. Enid, Oklahoma turned out to be the showplace for courtroom drama concerning their legal custody.

Oklahoma City became the venue for their mother's fight for her freedom. Her battle began the minute she stepped onto United States' soil from Mexico. Shortly after returning from Laredo to Oklahoma City, she and James spent their nights in the Oklahoma County Jail, in downtown Oklahoma City. On Friday, March 8, they appeared before a judge via a video for arraignment.

The Honorable Russell D. Hall was the Special Judge appointed to her case. Brenda's attorney's partner, George Miskovsky Jr., pled for her release on bail. Quiet, with her eyes downward, Brenda showed little emotion. Judge Hall had served Oklahoma County as a Special Judge since 1987. His docket had included more than 45,000 cases of arraignment per year. It was his job to monitor the jail population with assurance that timely charges be filed in criminal cases. District Attorney, Wes Lane, had filed first-degree murder charges against Brenda and James. Bail was denied. A preliminary hearing was set for April 15, 2002.

Brenda perked up when she got word that Greg McCracken

was in Garfield County in court. McCracken had earned a solid reputation in civil trial litigation. In particular, he excelled in divorce and custody cases. He had filed a motion for her family to gain guardianship of Genesee and Connor. Anxious for news from McCracken, she asked, "Will he call me back today?"

Miskovsky assured her that they would keep in touch.

Meanwhile, along with Brenda, James was denied bail. His attorney, Tom Cummings, had not appeared for his client before Judge Hall. Pavatt's preliminary hearing date could not be set until Cummings showed up.

Miskovsky maintained that his client could not possibly be guilty of killing her husband because no evidence had surfaced to that effect. He contended that Brenda's charge of guilt was only "by association."

March winds blew no respite for Brenda. She remained in the Oklahoma County Jail, able to talk with her children only by telephone. Brenda wanted them to live with her sister, Kim Bowlin. Rob's parents remained their temporary guardians, but Associate District Judge Richard Perry set a trial date of April 4 and 5, 2002 for the settlement. A psychologist would report at that time on the emotional state of the two Andrew children. For the present, they were not allowed to see or talk to Rose Evers. Brenda's attorneys were livid. Interviewed, Miskovsky implied that the Andrew grandparents had adopted a very 'cold' attitude toward Brenda's relatives. Implying that strangers were allowed to be with the children, but not their maternal grandmother, he berated them as acting un-Christian.

Delays were common for court proceedings. McCracken and his partners objected to everything brought to light by the prosecutor on their road to a preliminary hearing. Their obstacles blighted the D.A.'s path to a quick and just hearing.

When Pavatt's truck was impounded by the Oklahoma City Police, blood evidence had been detected. On April 16, 2002, Brenda and James sat together in court while their lawyers argued about testing the blood. The two defendants were each handcuffed but chatted together at the outset. Attorney Michael Arnett now acted for Pavatt. James had excused his former attorney after the bail hearing. Well-known in Oklahoma City as a former TV Channel 9 news reporter, Arnett stated that the couple were good friends and would not put one another in jeopardy by engaging in casual conversation.

Thirty-five minutes into the hearing, McCracken moved Brenda to the defense table. It was obvious that he was more comfortable with her sitting in close proximity. Lane's prosecutor, Fern Smith requested they be allowed full use of all blood smear samples from Pavatt's truck. She reported that samples were minuscule, too small to allow further testing.

McCracken voiced two concerns that day. He wanted independent DNA studies on the blood smears taken from an automatic bank machine receipt, an auto insurance form, a white envelope and one of Pavatt's business cards. He contended the defense should have access to the same testing as the prosecution.

McCracken's second major concern delayed a decision on the first. Judge Ray Elliott was docketed to become the trial judge for the two defendants. If he ruled early on the blood evidence, he would be compromised as a trial judge. His word on evidence could be seen as conflicted, for the actual trial. Due to McCracken's insistence, the blood analysis question was delayed until April 30.

The Honorable Ray C. Elliott had graduated from Oklahoma City University School of Law was employed as an Assistant District Attorney in Oklahoma County until 1998. Elected a District Judge for the County in 1999, he'd served as a trial judge in the Criminal Court Division ever since.

He was a "no-nonsense" jurist. His courtroom is a classic chamber, with polished furniture and meticulously vacuumed floors. It was rumored that, on occasion, the judge himself wielded the sweeper. At the Andrew/Pavatt hearing, Elliott stopped the proceedings when he heard the sound of gum or candy crackling.

"I'll not have anyone in my courtroom chewing gum or candy," he said. A brief recess allowed the offending person to spit out the unwanted item.

Further legal manipulations by both sides would delay the preliminary hearing several months, until June. McCracken moved to have the hearing and trial moved from Oklahoma City. That motion failed. Both Brenda and James would share a preliminary hearing. The inquiry would determine if there was sufficient evidence against them to proceed with a trial. Ray Elliott would hear the case.

However, McCracken threw a curve into the prosecution's quest for a trial. Ray Elliott's wife, Saundra Elliott, was an attorney in the D.A.'s office. She had been present when a committee of attorneys voted to bring murder charges against the two. Citing a major conflict of interest, McCracken managed a small coup against the judge's integrity. Now, another judge was appointed to preside at the preliminary trial.

Meanwhile, Brenda's days were monotonous. She was allowed an hour daily for exercise and a shower outside her narrow cell. She requested, and was granted, visits from jail chaplains, Christians trained to counsel inmates. Counsel was limited to concerns about religious matters; and how an inmate could learn to cope with separation from her family. In Brenda's case, she anguished over her lack of communication with her kids. Their welfare was foremost on her mind. In coming months, she completed Bible studies and read literature recommended for her spiritual growth.

During the early months of 2002, my exposure to Brenda's problems was limited. Media reported events as they unfolded. When the Andrew grandparents confronted Rose Evers about the kids' belongings, my emotions erupted. I began to question Brenda's role in their future care. No matter how courtroom litigation turned out, my sentiments shifted in favor of Rob's family.

CHAPTER 23

Enough for a Trial?

On May 3, 2002, I opened the mail. An official letter, addressed to Dean, subpoenaed him to testify before Judge Carol Hubbard, as a witness for the prosecution. Judge Hubbard had been selected by random pick to hear evidence for Brenda and James' preliminary hearings. The legal language, including the word, *COMMANDED*, typed in capital letters, made my skin tingle.

Another letter came the following day, requiring Dean to set up an appointment with District Attorney, C. Wesley Lane II, to discuss his testimony. The purpose was to determine whether or not a crime had "probably" occurred and whether or not there was evidence that the defendant "probably" committed the crime. If Judge Hubbard found sufficient evidence, the next step would be a trial.

I breathed a sigh of relief that I was not called to testify. By that time I had agreed write a book about the murder and its consequences. I needed to hear every proceeding, every bit of testimony. If I were called as a witness, I would not be able to attend trial sessions until after giving my testimony.

Dean would make a better witness than I. He was gifted with a feel for numbers, sequence of events and a timing that I don't possess. Emotion, not reason, would dictate my testimony.

I was doubly glad for the pass when Dean received a subpoena from the defendant's attorney a few days later. A call to the District Attorney's office confirmed that the procedure was normal; cross-subpoenas to cover all the bases. I phoned our neighbor, Bee

Jay Garrison,who confirmed that he had received a double sub-poena as well. A check for ten dollars accompanied the one from Brenda's attorneys, for Dean's expenses. He cashed it. If it had come to me, I would have been squeamish to take the money

An hour early, on June 5, accompanied by my daughter-in-law, Sarah Gigstad, I arrived at Judge Carol Hubbard's courtroom on the 5th floor of the Oklahoma County courthouse. On the first day of preliminary hearings, we wanted to make certain we would have a seat. Brenda's mother, sister and husband, aunt and uncle and Kim's teenage daughter moved toward the door while we waited on a bench outside. Rose and Kim talked, wondering aloud whether cameras would be allowed in the courtroom.

The court clerk opened the door, and the drama began. We filed in and took seats. Brenda's family sat on the front rows, directly behind the table where she would be seated. The attor-neys for both sides took their places. Two lawyers, Mike Arnett and his assistant, represented Pavatt. Brenda's divorce attorney Greg McCracken and Frank Miskovsky II, and Miskovsky III, along with two assistants filled Brenda's table. I wondered where they would squeeze in the two defendants. The two lead detectives, Roland Garrett and Gary Damron sat down at the prosecutor's table, alongside Wes Lane and Fern Smith. Bill and Tom Andrew joined them to represent the victim. Lane spoke with the two Andrew brothers outside the courtroom before events began. Outside the chamber, a noisy commotion added to the tension.

TV lights filtered through windows in the courtroom doors. The television cameramen from local news stations had positioned themselves for a good view of the defendants when they left the 5th floor elevator. Uniformed sheriff's deputies escorted Brenda and James into the courtroom. Both wore orange jail-issue jumpsuits, clean but badly fit. When the elevator door closed be-hind them, the cameras droned. The media would make sure to capture a good front-page picture.

When Brenda and James entered the courtroom, I was struck by the clanking of their hand and leg shackles, like loose chains banging against a flag pole in the wind. Captive, and awaiting her fate, Brenda looked straight ahead and didn't acknowledge family or friends. When she took her seat beside her attorneys, she tossed her long black hair aside. Without care, the roots of her hair showed a lighter, brown color. For the former homeroom mom and Sunday school teacher, the embarrassment must have been brutal.

I was struck by the mountain of legal papers that covered the defendants' tables. Finally, the court clerk introduced Judge Carol Hubbard and all stood. When the case number and names were announced, three or four persons left the room. Apparently, word had not reached other defendants that Judge Hubbard would not hear their cases. Court dockets bulged for the Special Circuit Judges. Judge Hubbard struck me as far too young to hear such an important indictment. The attractive blond judge looked like a recent college graduate, not a seasoned jurist. Her opening words didn't fill me with confidence.

She said, "You'll have to bear with me. I'm the new kid on the block."

Later, I heard from the D.A.'s assistant, Jenny Fowler, that Judge Hubbard had recently been appointed to hear preliminary trial cases on the court docket. However, her experience on the bench was substantial and her qualifications without question. I breathed easier.

McCracken requested that Enid Attorney Box be asked to leave, as he might later be called as a potential witness. However, the State released him from testimony, thus allowing him to remain in the room. The two lead detectives were also given the right to stay. Attorneys requested that the defendants' hand shackles be removed, and it was granted. Legal, but necessary maneuverings.

Shortly before 10:00 A.M., the first witness was called. William "Stanley" Morgan was sworn in, and Brenda's reputation began a downhill spiral.

In mid-life, Stanley was a tall, handsome dark-haired man with an easy smile. He described his first meeting with Brenda. She was a customer in the grocery store he managed in November 1999. Dressed in low-cut top and short mini-skirt, she had talked and flirted with him for more than three weeks. In the first or second week of December she had slipped him a motel room key with an invitation to meet her that afternoon. McCracken stood up and objected to this line of questioning, but was overruled.

Morgan continued. He and Brenda had had sex in the motel at least twice a week until May, 2001. He called her daily until the affair ended. *She* paid for the motel room. When asked what had ended their sexual relationship he replied, "She said that I had changed, and it wasn't fun anymore."

Despite having no further sex, the couple had remained friends. Brenda hired Morgan and his two college-age sons to paint her dining room, house exterior, to replace a dilapidated fence and build another fence between her house and ours. He also replaced the backyard decking outside her kitchen door, complete with staircases and railings. In all, he was on the Andrew property at least seventy-five times.

During the summer, Morgan had met Pavatt. James had bragged about his past dangerous work assignments in the armed services. Morgan overheard Pavatt mention that he had "killed more than once, but he'd only missed one time."

The questioning shifted to the Andrew marriage. Morgan listened to her say that her husband was verbally abusive, that she hated him and wanted a divorce. She had wished him dead so that she wouldn't have to endure a divorce. However, she had not asked Morgan to kill Rob. When he finally met Rob at the end of the summer, his impression of an abusive man had changed. Rob appeared to be a good man and caring father. Morgan quoted Brenda. "She wished him (Rob) dead…" Brenda wanted money to provide for the kids without her going to work.

He reported that she also had told him about problems at the church in May, 2001, complaining of gossip about the way she dressed. Church leaders had asked her and Pavatt to resign from teaching their sixth-grade class. Now, she felt uncomfortable continuing to attend services at North Pointe.

The last chore Morgan had done for Brenda was on November 20. She'd called and asked him to help Pavatt unload a washer and dryer. In addition, Morgan kept her company while she packed clothing the kids would take with them for Thanksgiving with Rob. She selected four of each item, matching the number of days away from home.

Previously, Morgan had been a character witness for Brenda in her divorce hearing. Along with her other friends, he thought she'd been preoccupied with an insurance policy covering Rob and naming her as beneficiary. Rob wanted the kids to be beneficiaries, but Brenda had argued against it. Morgan and Brenda's additional witnesses had thought she overreacted. In either case, the kids would still benefit.

Morgan explained that he had told his wife about the affair the day after the murder. Seated on the front row during his testimony, Patty Morgan distracted her husband with eye contact. Noting the diversion, Judge Hubbard asked her to leave.

On cross-examination, McCracken asked him about the divorce hearing and his opinion of the settlement. Morgan was asked why he confessed the affair to his wife. McCracken zeroed in on times, dates and sequences of events. In addition, Brenda had flirted with his sons during the work on the deck, an unnecessary intrusion. He had also seen pages of Rob's journal in the living room and noticed loose sheets scattered on the floor.

McCracken asked Morgan if he'd been the second shooter at the murder scene. He replied, emphatically, "No!" When asked about Pavatt, Morgan's opinion was that James was a bullshitter. He didn't trust or like the man.

The first morning of the hearing ground to a lunch time halt. A break from courtroom drama was needed, respite for minds bogged with testimony. Each day during the proceedings, the judge instructed us not to talk about the case during breaks. The oddity was that the majority of those involved spent the noon hour at a food court in the lower level of a building adjoining the courthouse. Sarah and I sat in a corner, away from Brenda's gregarious attorneys. We people-watched, digesting what we'd heard that morning but careful to avoid discussing the testimony.

CHAPTER 24

Reputations Sullied

In the afternoon, Pavatt's attorney, Arnett, drilled Morgan on statements made earlier. Skillful at twisting testimony, Arnett tried to make him appear the shunned lover, jealous enough to be involved in murder. But he was not successful. I thought Arnett bullied his witness.

Revelations of Brenda's sexual exploits continued with the next witness, Rick Nunley. His ex-wife had worked with Brenda at her bank job, and the two couples had been friends. He confessed to having intimate relations with Brenda from the fall of 1997 until spring, 1998, while both were married. While he talked about the affair, I remembered a conversation we'd had with the Andrews in the summer of 1998. We had drunk beer together on their deck and made small talk. Rob told us about friends of theirs who were having marital problems, an alleged infidelity on the husband's part. Little did he dream then that it was Brenda having the affair with Rick. Now, Rick's testimony clarified the facts. He and his wife subsequently divorced.

Nunley had talked with Brenda about her divorce situation two weeks before Thanksgiving, 2001. She had confided that Rob tried to change the insurance policy. She was angry when Rob had taken sides against her and James at the church. She'd confided in Rick as a friend, he testified.

Nunley first learned of the murder the next morning when Brenda called him and said, "Rob and I were shot last night. Rob's dead."

She told him the same details of the shooting she'd told the police. Then she mentioned the insurance policy and its contested ownership. They talked again Thursday night when Nunley was in Tulsa. He asked for more details about the shooting, but she was not specific. She insisted that only one of the shooters had a gun. When she left Rob's side to call 911, he was still breathing and mumbling. Nunley reported that he had not heard from Brenda again until she was in custody in Texas. She'd called him at home and asked him to pick up important documents, including a written confession from the children's suitcases, and get them to her sister, mother or attorney.

She had implored him, "I need those papers in the hands of my relatives."

Cross-examination covered the same points. McCracken grilled Nunley on Brenda's character, whether or not she was capable of killing Rob. Rick presented her as a loving mother. She'd leaned on him for support after the shooting. He continually denied that Brenda asked him to help her kill Rob. She'd written five letters to him from jail. Pavatt's team asked the same questions over and over. I felt as if it was I who had been drilled.

Observing the proceedings, I was struck by the enormity of their importance. The question of a murder trial hung on the balance of testimony given here. I wanted to believe in the innocence of my neighbor, but Brenda's actions pointed in a dire direction. Witnesses continued to smear her reputation.

Bill Andrew, Rob's 43-year old brother, told of his conversation with Rob prior to the forthcoming Thanksgiving holiday, in 2001. The Friday before, they talked about going hunting over the holiday weekend. Bill had asked Rob to bring his shotgun, a 16-guage that he'd owned since his teenage years. Rob had asked Brenda to get it from his closet at the house, but she refused. Citing Rob's uneasiness after the brake line incident, Bill said that his brother feared James might do him harm.

Ron Stump, Rob's best friend, was the next witness for the prosecution. He recounted Rob's exasperation with the church situation. Rob had told him that he did not agree with James and Brenda's dismissal. It had hurt all of them and did not solve he problem of her infidelity. Ron had witnessed the angry confrontation between Rob and James outside the church on September 19.

His advice to Rob was to back away from further contact until things cooled down.

Stump related that he had remained Rob's close confidant after he had moved into an apartment. Rob was diligent about attending their early morning Bible study group five days a week. He'd kept close phone contact with Rob until his death. At times, Rob had talked about Brenda's harassment. She'd accused Rob of having an affair. Finally, Rob had taped conversations with her.

On cross-examination, Stump admitted that he had never seen James with Rob's gun. Nor had he seen Rob carry the gun out of their house. But when Rob and Stump had returned to Rob's apartment the night they had tried to see Lacey's new puppy, Rob had said, "I feel as if a gun is on me." Stump admitted that he had not heard either Brenda or James threaten Rob. Further cross-examination concerned Ron's knowledge of the cut brake-lines in late October. However, Stump contended that Rob's focus was on his marriage and a possible reconciliation with Brenda.

Ralph Burnett, James' boss at Prudential Life Insurance Co., testified about the telephone call he had with Rob Andrew about his life insurance policy. On October 30, 2001, Rob requested a beneficiary change to his brother, Tom Andrew. When questioned about the policy, James had insisted that Brenda was now the owner *and* policy beneficiary. Further correspondence between the company and Rob would be relayed to the agent of record, James Pavatt. Papers he produced showed that Brenda had become owner of the policy on March 22, 2001. Burnett's testimony now centered on paperwork discrepancies. Additional questions about the policy would be forwarded to the agency's home office.

At this point in the proceedings, I noticed that Judge Hubbard looked tired. We all squirmed in the hard wooden seats. On the third day, Pavatt's ex-wife, SukHui, would be heard. Following questions to establish her identity and relevance to the accused, she overcame initial discomfort. She had sat, crying and looking terrified of the entire process. Now, she talked about money problems in her marriage to James. In August, 2001, he had convinced her to return to Korea, where his previous secret duties in the army could not harm her. Trusting him, she signed divorce papers mailed to her there. Brenda's credit card was charged with SukHui's airfare. In October, Pavatt convinced her to return to Oklahoma City, to reconcile. They had kept close contact during the fall. She had lent him her '92 Beretta on the Sunday following Rob's death. He said that the media would hound his white truck, hoping for an interview. He denied any part in Rob's killing. She believed him.

When they exchanged vehicles, he loaded a military duffle bag and a black gun case into her trunk. When asked if they had talked again or if she had gotten her car back, she replied, "No."

Testimony from Detective Mike Klicka centered on Rob's police report made when his brake lines had been cut. The detective recounted conversations with the Nissan dealer's service manager. Rob's description of the day's events, from severed brake lines to the calls urging him to go to the Norman Hospital, supported fears that his life was in danger. Detective Klicka's report was now in the D.A.'s possession.

Roger Frost was on duty as a Security Officer for Lansbrook the night of November 20, 2001. His testimony covered the 911 call of a home invasion on Shaftsbury. He recalled Brenda's demeanor once he arrived at the residence and her subsequent behavior when he accompanied her to the hospital. He had experienced reactions from several hundred victims of violent crimes. Hers, he said, was unusual. She appeared too calm, and her cry about her wounded arm fake.

The defense tried to compromise Frost's testimony. Attorneys forced him to concede that Brenda had willingly cooperated when questioned by detectives, both at home and at the hospital.

When SukHui was on the stand, Brenda shot understanding looks at her. SukHui composed herself from tears by touching a handkerchief to her cheek, while smiling at James. Watching Detective Klicka, Brenda's demeanor was smug. I was curious how she'd react to Dean's deposition. During the hearings, Sarah observed all participants and noted their reactions.

Dean was sworn in and described our acquaintance with the Andrews. He made the point, when asked, that we had been friends, not close but casual enough to exchange house keys when we traveled. The account of items both misplaced, broken and missing, when we returned from Kansas after Thanksgiving, took a large block of time. Additional comments covered his conversation with Brenda during her divorce proceedings, in addition to Pavatt's increasing appearances at her house. Dean identified

Pavatt as owner of the white Ford 150 truck. He described the spent shotgun shell we found in a bedroom overlooking the Andrew's deck, and how we had tried to contact police that night.

The defense tried to discredit Dean by inferring that we did not actually see anyone enter our attic or the spare bedroom. Anyone could have broken into our house. Dean had not heard Brenda threaten to kill Rob. Dean was badgered, but the defense had a case to make.

The prosecution's most intimidating witness was Janna Larson, Pavatt's daughter. She recounted her history with Brenda, as James' friend. In early October, she asked him about the relationship. He had replied that Brenda had only been sexual with her husband. Later, that month, he told Jana about plans to marry Brenda after her divorce was final, by the next summer. They wanted to have a child together.

Questions followed about Janna's involvement with Brenda's bank account, in Norman. The account information was mailed to Pavatt's P.O. Box. She testified about being the caller requesting Rob to drive to the Norman Hospital the day his brake lines were cut. Her father had denied knowledge of the cut lines. He also denied involvement in Rob's murder. In fact, he'd borrowed Janna's car to go fishing that evening.

But when Pavatt and Brenda turned up missing, Janna had contacted the FBI, on her mother's advice. She worried about possible charges against her, if she'd been used in a scheme against Rob. She had seen a firearm in Pavatt's apartment in November and asked him about it. It was a recent purchase, for his protection. Janna noticed a bullet on the front floorboard when James returned her car. Alarmed, she called her father.

"Throw it away," he told her. "Don't tell anyone about it."

Instead, she kept the bullet.

The remaining witnesses renewed the state's claims of sufficient evidence to warrant a trial. Police spokesperson, Theresa Bunn, owner of a gun shop where Pavatt had purchased a pistol was questioned and cross-examined. During Bunn's cross, the judge ordered Miskovsky III to quit treating her as a hostile witness.

Finally, when no further witnesses were called, Judge Hubbard ruled that the prosecution had presented sufficient evidence to go to trial. The legal sparring had just begun. Along with Rob's family, I was relieved that Oklahoma County could proceed with the indictments.

CHAPTER 25

Appealing

Months dragged, and the move toward justice slowed to turtle's pace. Following the Preliminary Hearing I had reconciled with losing Judge Elliott as trial arbitrator. Brenda's attorneys argued he had a solid conflict of interest. Elliott's wife, Saundra, was an assistant prosecutor for the D.A. She had signed paperwork charging the pair with murder. I puzzled why Pavatt's attorney did not request Elliott's removal at the time. Meanwhile, McCracken hammered on the personal conflict issue. Judge Elliott stepped down, opening the door for Judge Susan Bragg.

Arnett maintained Pavatt's right to a speedy trial. A scant three weeks after capture, legal maneuvers dampened that hope. Court etiquette in a double murder case maintains the District Attorney's right to decide the order of trials. Wes Lane was quoted saying that "the first would likely be James Pavatt."

For close to a half hour, District Judge Susan Bragg met with Brenda's four attorneys behind closed doors. McCracken convinced her to try Brenda and Pavatt in separate proceedings. The hearing protected them from sharing plans with Pavatt's counsel or the prosecutors. By that time, the ambiance between the defendants appeared to splinter. Judge Bragg decided that the evidence was sufficient for two trials.

A previous assessment implied the need for six weeks for a joint trial. Now, time estimates appeared murky. The major participants for prosecution and the defendants' attorneys attracted the media. The judge's calendar, jury selection and witness subpoenas would each factor into the period allotted for each trial.

Judge Elliott's calendar had allowed for Pavatt's trial to begin in late January. Bragg's docket, however, was filled until summer. McCracken jammed a log in the road by filing an appeal. Judge Bragg scheduled the trials to begin in Oklahoma City in June.

"Overwhelming pre-trial publicity will taint the process," attorneys stated. "There will be no way Andrew and Pavatt can get a fair trial in Oklahoma County."

McCracken's appeal to the Oklahoma Court of Criminal Appeals asked Judge Bragg to move Brenda's trial out of Oklahoma County. In late January, he backed his request with a dramatic presentation.

Three individuals unfurled and upheld a large roll of brown paper before the court. Seventy-four newspaper articles from the pages of *The Daily Oklahoman* delivered McCracken's message. Loni Shropshire, marketing development manager at the newspaper, identified page numbers and evidence of a photo with each story. McCracken cited that 40 articles to date had been front page stories, read by 93 percent of readers.

Mrs. Fern Smith, lead prosecutor, stressed that Brenda's attorneys failed to present a single prospective Oklahoma County juror who would be unfair. She made clear that the law allows citizens to serve as jurors, despite media and newspaper circulation, but they must base a verdict solely on trial evidence.

Judge Bragg concurred with the prosecution at this point. She said, "Not until such time we bring in a large panel...*voire dire* them – that's the only way to make that determination."

She upheld their right to be questioned in jury selection, with attorneys having the right to select or dismiss. Despite Andrew's appeal, the trial remained in Oklahoma County.

I read the news story and had a good laugh. The "cut and paste" technique, common in elementary schools, had invaded the courtroom as well.

Media flooded the airways with news about the pair's legal issues. Stalemates crippled hope for speedy trials. Images of mounting dollar costs fluttered into my mind.

From brighter times, I remembered Genesee and Connor dressed in Halloween costumes on my doorstep. Now, they deserved a nurturing home. I clung to hopes for their happiness in Enid, with the Andrew family.

An Enid courtroom provided the setting for continued crisis. E.R. and Lou Andrew filed motions for the children's guardianship in mid-February, 2003. Brenda's sister, Kim Bowlin, cast a dark shadow by seeking guardianship as well. Garfield County Associate District Judge Richard M. Perry heard testimony for three days while eight witnesses supported the Bowlin claims. Before testimony concluded, the judge would confer with the children. McCracken represented Bowlin, for Brenda. Her influence impacted the process at every turn. The court appointed a separate attorney, Phil Outhier, to oversee the children's interests.

I concluded that McCracken must lead the life of a jackrabbit, hopping up and down the Oklahoma highways. Kim's legal action squelched my hopes for the kids' return to normalcy. They made six visits to Brenda in the Oklahoma County jail during her first month there. Outhier told the court that the trips to jail stressed the children but he understood her right to see them.

Based on the furniture incident outside our house, I sympathized with Rob's family in the custody case. I knew that frustration over her daughter's arrest discouraged Rose Evers, but infighting between the grandparents would only hurt the children. Outhier conceded that when scheduling at the jail allowed, the kids could visit their mother. McCracken stressed that Brenda had never been declared an unfit mother. He remained certain that the children would tell the judge that they wanted to live with Jim and Kim Bowlin.

The judge stood firm. He would not be hurried; time and testimony would dictate his ruling. While the winter's ice melted, psychologists were expert witnesses for both sides in the case.

Assuming that Brenda's trial would begin within weeks after a Pavatt verdict, Judge Perry rendered his judgment. Meanwhile, the Andrew children would remain in the custody of Rob's parents, with visits arranged for the Bowlin and Evers side. The verdict in Brenda's trial would determine the final guardianship.

My confidence in the court system was upheld. The Andrew kids would be scarred from their recent emotional trauma, but loving grandparents, together with uncle, aunts and cousins, would help heal the wounds. I applauded their efforts.

Media coverage stoked the flames under a simmering kettle, a stew-pot of facts. The ingredients that were James Pavatt's defense would soon enter the test kitchen, ripe for stirring.

CHAPTER 26

Pavatt's Day in Court

For months following the pair's arrest, Brenda's attorney held a crucial document, a confession alleged to have been written by Pavatt. McCracken was supposed to have obtained the letter from Kim Bowlin in Hidalgo, Texas. The clock ticked toward Pavatt's trial date in June.

Late in May, Mike Arnett, together with the state's attorneys, made an appearance before Judge Bragg to secure the letter. McCracken's team insisted that its content would exonerate Brenda. Arnett argued that the Pavatt family lacked money to pay handwriting experts for analysis. Additional time, to sell family property, would be required.

Arnett maintained, "...A critical piece of evidence...changes my whole defense."

Back in February McCracken had used the letter to fuel requests for separate trials. Three weeks prior to their arrest, McCracken had notified the District Attorney that the letter existed. He would hand it over to the D.A. in return for dismissal of the charges. At the time Lane contended that the confession appeared to be invented. Prosecutors argued that McCracken's refusal had crushed hopes for a short trial. Arnett's defense that his client was not at the crime scene would suffer from a confession.

Judge Bragg's ruling, "...Defense ordered to turn over the letter by 5:00 P.M. Tuesday," narrowed the playing field for Pavatt's defense. She ruled to delay his trial by three months, sufficient time for the document's examination.

Jury selection would begin on Monday, August 25, 2003.

Now, summer heat baked Oklahoma while advocates for both sides of the case gathered mountains of paper, along with audio and video evidence.

Dean once again received a summons from the District Attorney's office to testify. One afternoon prior to his appointment with prosecutors, I answered the door. A courier delivered a certified letter for Dean, accompanied by a check. Now, he had been subpoenaed by the defense. Considering his previous testimony, I questioned how Pavatt's team could consider him anything but a hostile witness.

Dean discovered that it was common practice to cross-subpoena witnesses in a capital case. The defense would bank on confusing the witness and wrenching statements favorable for their own client. At best, they might influence the jury to favor the defendant.

Pavatt's counsel attempted another delay. They hadn't received a report on the confession letter. According to Arnett, there was not sufficient time before trial to analyze and possibly contest the findings of the state's expert handwriting witness. Arnett argued further that the *Oklahoman* had published enough statements about the letter to prejudice a jury. Judge Bragg refused a continuance.

On August 25, a jury pool of one hundred persons was summoned to the Oklahoma County Court. Twenty-seven were dismissed in the first two days for various reasons: disbelief in the death penalty, refusal to give a sentence of life without parole, pre-trial opinions, acquaintance with Brenda's daughter, death in the family, medical reasons, and felony conviction. Following questions by the defense, thirty prospective jurors remained. Each side could excuse nine, with twelve remaining seated to decide Pavatt's fate. Prior to opening arguments, two alternates would be chosen.

The final panel consisted of nine women and three men, their average age between thirty and thirty-five. Their backgrounds were diverse, from retail sales, construction industry, medical personnel, communications work, stay-at-home parent, service industry workers and students, to a small business owner.

The prosecution was reported to have called more than sixty witnesses while the defense assembled half that number.

I knew several of Arnett's witnesses to be double-subpoenaed. This ploy would keep them from the courtroom during other testimony. Dean would have to sit outside the chamber until he had appeared for both sides. Our son, Jeff, also was issued a summons for the defense. However, his wife, Sarah and I were allowed into the courtroom. Based on experience in the preliminary hearing, we'd curb urges to flash signals to them.

Janna Larson, handwriting analysts, forensics experts, detectives and Pavatt's boss from Prudential Insurance Company were additional witnesses. Although Janna had cooperated with the FBI while Pavatt and Andrew hid in Mexico, she now leaned toward her father's defense. A flip-flop could destroy her credibility for either side. Outside the courtroom, she blew kisses to her dad when he was escorted from the jail elevator by two uniformed officers. No longer in leg shackles, he wore business attire, with white shirt and tie, appearing as a well-dressed executive.

The judge admonished us about conversations outside the courtroom. No discussion of the case was allowed. Judge Bragg threatened severe penalties if her orders were abused.

Chief prosecutor, Fern Smith, opened the prosecution's case with the statement, "This case is about a controlling wife and her lover, James Pavatt."

Arnett countered by saying that no evidence would surface incriminating Pavatt . Taking Andrew to Mexico had been a huge mistake but not proof of his guilt.

Following Arnett's opening remarks, prosecutors called witnesses to testify against Pavatt.

Early in the trial the confession letter loomed as a pivotal point. David Parrett, a handwriting expert, testified for the D.A. that Pavatt *did* write the letter to Andrew's daughter. Though undated, it implicated Pavatt and an unidentified friend as having planned and executed Rob's murder. He wrote that he intended to remove Rob from Brenda's life. He feared the Andrews would reconcile after Thanksgiving. He described the murder event in detail, taking full blame. On the trip to Mexico, Pavatt had confessed the crime to Brenda. Shocked by his action, she was angry. He apologized to Genesee for their bickering. The final lines reinforced his love for her and her brother. He confided that the children did not miss their father, nor did they love him. The letter was signed, "Love, Jim."

When Janna Larson took the stand for the prosecution, she was adamant that her father had not written the letter. She implied that Andrew's attorneys had pieced the composition together from thirteen letters she had previously turned over to the FBI. But Parrett had testified that it could not have been a cut-and-paste document because the ink used throughout was consistent. Prosecutors channeled the handwriting analyst's witness in a second important direction. Brenda Andrew was named as both owner and beneficiary of Rob's Life Insurance Policy for $800,000.00. Parrett had compared Rob's signature on the document to 136 others on numerous documents he'd signed. The expert's analysis further substantiated a motive for Rob's murder. Greed became a huge factor.

The spectators sat upright and leaned forward in anticipation. Several jurors were taking notes. Parrett indicated points in Rob's signature that were specific to his style. The policy appeared a forgery.

In fact, previous testimony by Pavatt's boss, Ralph Burnett, verified that James had submitted paperwork to change the ownership of Rob Andrew's $800,000.00 life insurance policy to Brenda Andrew. When Rob suspected that the ownership had changed, he contacted Burnett. Rob told Burnett that he wanted to set up a trust on the policy for his children. He named his brother, Tom Andrew, as the trustee. However, at the time of his death, that trust had not been implemented.

Burnett testified, "I checked on the computer and Rob was in fact the owner. Jim said he'd submitted the paperwork to Prudential to have the ownership changed."

Prosecutors hammered the fact that the insurance papers submitted to his company did not include Rob Andrew's signature. In addition, Prudential's telephone records supported conflicting reports on the policy's ownership. The prosecution submitted five audiotapes listing calls made between September 24, 2001 and November 2, 2001. After his brake lines were cut, Rob insisted that his life was in danger.

In one phone call to Prudential, he had stated, "There was an attempt on my life today...I think my agent is in cahoots with my wife to get the policy."

Brenda and James claimed that ownership of the policy had changed on March 22, 2001. She was not only the owner but beneficiary. Pavatt said that the date on the form was March 22, 2000, a full year earlier. At that time, he had inserted an entry in Rob's file about the change of ownership.

Burnett recalled that Pavatt had inquired at the corporate level about the change. Brenda, by telephone, had accused Prudential of making a mistake and angrily called the company to correct the papers. She bombarded the agency with accusations.

The jurors followed Burnett's testimony with intensity. The majority listened closely, digesting the meat of each statement. Rob's insistence that he had not signed the change of ownership was upheld by testimony from his divorce lawyer, Craig L. Box. According to Box, Rob was 75% certain he didn't sign the papers dated March 22, 2001.

Box testified, "I remember distinctly, Rob said she (Brenda) bragged to him that she could sign his name better than him."

Cramped, with our brains overloaded from the mountains of evidence, we welcomed a break in the testimony. Sarah and I dined in the food court where both prosecution and defense attorneys ate. The same uneasiness accompanied us that we'd experienced during the preliminary hearings, but whispers about courtroom proceedings were strictly taboo.

CHAPTER 27
Pavatt's Day Resumes

Following a lunch break, the drama resumed. The prosecution continued to focus on the fight for the $800,000.00 insurance policy. Money as the motive topped their list. When Pavatt's office manager was excused, prosecutors called Lawrence Frotten to the stand. Frotten had accumulated 22 years of experience with Prudential, the last six years as manager of investigations. He established the time frame for when Pavatt had requested a Change of Ownership form on Rob's policy. His records showed that Pavatt faxed the document to the home office on 10-29-2001. However, the form showed a signature dated 3-22-2001.

Prudential's policy dictates that when an ownership change is requested, the agent of record verifies with the insured via a letter of confirmation. Frotten testified that no such letter had been sent out. Prosecutors next submitted the log of calls Prudential received from Rob, following his brake line scare on 10-29-2001. By telephone, he had requested a change naming his brother, Tom his beneficiary on the policy.

To further complicate the issue, Frotten's testimony revealed Brenda Andrew had called Prudential multiple times. She had argued with a receptionist named Jennifer about the "wrong information" on policy ownership and beneficiary. Adamant that change papers had been posted in March, 2001, Brenda insisted that her husband was "doing crazy things" regarding the insurance. At fever pitch, she implied that Prudential was working from incorrect information. She charged the staff to "call her back and tell her it's done." The information was to be directed both to her cell phone and her lawyer. More than once, an angry Brenda had slammed the phone on Prudential's office workers. Conflicting dates regarding the change papers, angry phone calls from Pavatt, Brenda and Rob, and lack of log data failed to prove or disprove Brenda's claims. Prosecutors persevered the "greed" motive.

Brenda Andrew's two previous boyfriends corroborated that she disliked her husband. While both remained friends with Brenda following the end of sexual relationships with her, both had met James Pavatt. Stanley Morgan said that Pavatt bragged about his army duties: "Top-secret, dangerous work" and "killing people for a living."

Morgan recalled his appearance in support of Brenda at her divorce hearing. His puzzled look expressed his feelings. At the time, he had failed to understand her obsession with the life insurance policy ownership.

On November 20, 2001, Brenda's six-foot "friend, Stanley" had helped her much shorter "friend, James" load a washer into his truck at her house. That day, Brenda had not mentioned that the furnace pilot light was on the blink. She did not ask either of them to look at or re-light it. If the furnace was malfunctioning, Morgan could not recall being cold or uncomfortable inside the house.

While working on the deck earlier in September, Morgan had helped Rob carry personal items and clothing out to a truck when the couple separated. At the time he'd observed a shotgun in Rob's closet. He recognized it as a single-shot, break-apart weapon.

He had said to Rob, "You should put that up away from the kids, if they're going to be around."

Hearing this account, I saw that a murder weapon had indeed emerged. The idea collected substance with the next witness.

Ron Stump, Rob's best friend, expanded upon his testimony from the preliminary hearing. In casual conversation at church, Pavatt had boasted to Ron about his "special forces service and military police" experiences. Proudly, he stated that he had been in Desert Storm and had killed people on a secret mission for the military police.

Questioned further, Ron verified the sequence of events on the day that Rob's brake lines were cut. He and Rob had spoken repeatedly that day. Even more powerful in witness for the prosecution, he repeated the final conversation with Rob. Andrew had pulled into the driveway at 6112 Shaftsbury to pick up his kids for the upcoming Thanksgiving holiday.

He tape rolled. "Hi, buddy. I'm ready for a great time with my kids. . . . The garage door is going up. Looks like they're coming out now. Catch you later. . . "

Listening to Ron's account, members of both jury and the audience sat transfixed. I, too, digested their importance. Rob Andrew would be but a memory moments after their conversation. We needed a breather but prosecutors called their next witness.

Sukhui Pavatt took the stand. A sharp contrast to a confident Ron Stump, the tiny Korean woman seemed nervous. His former wife reinforced Pavatt's boasting about his military service. He told her that he had been drafted into Special Forces because he was good at shooting. In the summer of 2001, he convinced her that they needed to divorce, for her protection. People from his past "Special Forces life" were still trying to kill him. She could become caught in the middle. At his request, Sukhui flew back home to Korea. The marriage had been shaky for a time because Pavatt's daughter, Janna, seemed unable to accept Sukhui as stepmother. Their close age proximity posed an impossible hurdle. Besides, Janna adored her own mother, Pavatt's first wife. Money problems tarnished Jim and Sukhui's marriage further. Credit card debt had risen to an unmanageable level.

Sukhui may have seemed a fragile waif but she was a credible witness. Pavatt had duped her into a hasty divorce. They had maintained contact, despite her return to Korea. Brenda Andrew's credit card had covered the cost of her plane ticket.

But a twist occurred late in the summer of 2001. Pavatt convinced Sukhui to return to Oklahoma City. He talked about getting back together to make their marriage work. He said that Brenda Andrew intended to reunite with her husband. Sukhui was convinced that James was serious. His spiritual life seemed to be crumbling and he needed her help.

Devoutly religious, Sukhui had not felt uncomfortable in Pavatt's church. When he and Brenda stepped down from their teaching positions, he told Sukhui that he "didn't believe in God anymore." His ex-wife thought his attitude was harsh. She encouraged him to "come back to God."

When Sukhui returned to Oklahoma City, she felt that James had changed. She testified, "Something was not right for him."

He picked her up in Dallas, but during the entire drive back to Oklahoma City, he avoided conversation. Instead, he chatted on his cell phone. Laughing at times, it was clear that he was talking to Brenda Andrew.

Sukhui stated that shortly before Thanksgiving Pavatt had wanted to be alone, to sort things out. He planned to go fishing at Lake Thunderbird. She was unconcerned because his attitude had been strange since her return. He had seemed preoccupied with Brenda Andrew's situation despite his promises concerning their life together.

Following Rob's death, Pavatt had denied being involved in the crime. He did mention that he would stand by Brenda during a press conference. In that way, they would clear up any misinformation that the police might have. He arranged to borrow Sukhui's 1992 Chevrolet Beretta for the media interview before Rob's funeral on Monday. On Sunday, Sukhui met him and exchanged vehicles in a parking lot on Interstate 44, at a Buy For Less grocery store. Even under intense cross-examination, her recall did not waiver.

The trial moved forward with a storybook flow. Prosecuting attorneys demonstrated a clear progression of evidence pointing to a logical conclusion. Smith and her team brought witnesses in close proximity to the accused.

Pavatt's daughter, Janna, presented a marked change in attitude from her testimony at the preliminary hearing. There, she had willingly cooperated with the FBI. She now appeared to have a change of heart. When waiting outside the court chamber for her father, she had blown kisses his way and mouthed, "Daddy, I love you."

Between the preliminary hearing and Pavatt's trial, Janna's mother had died. Janna now supported her remaining parent.

Smith pressed her to admit that Brenda had deposited a little over $82,000.00 in a money market account at the Norman bank where Janna worked. Pavatt had warned her not to tell Rob about the account.

Pavatt had admitted a sexual relationship with Brenda and a disdain for her husband. At his apartment, Janna witnessed the stolen kisses in the kitchen, apart from the kids. That summer she asked her father about the involvement.

"He said that he and Brenda were going to have a baby together after she divorced her husband," Janna said. "I asked him about the kids telling their father. He (Pavatt) replied 'No, Brenda has them well trained.'"

Mrs. Smith plunged ahead with questions about Janna's car. On November 20, 2001, Pavatt had asked to swap vehicles with his daughter, for a fishing trip. He had told her that Brenda talked about getting back together with Rob. Pavatt had decided "get drunk and go fishing by himself at Lake Thunderbird."

At this point Janna flip-flopped on answers she had given under oath in the preliminary hearing. She had discovered a bullet on the passenger side floorboard of her car. When she had asked Pavatt about it, he told her to throw it away. She waffled on the time frame her car had been returned to her parking space.

Mrs. Smith's demeanor had been quiet, direct and matter-of-fact. Her next question sparked with anger.

"Miss Larson," she asked. "Which story is the truth, what you say today or the sworn testimony you gave in the preliminary hearing?"

We could have heard a pin drop. The change in Smith's tactic elicited the desired response. Her credibility questioned, Janna replied that whatever she had said at first must be the proper answer. But now her voice was subdued; a direct opposite of her earlier confidence.

The bullet's origin became a hazy recollection. Despite the fact that, on the advice of her lawyer, she had given it to the police, she admitted showing the silver bullet to her grandparents. It resembled ones they stored in an ammunition box. She had compared it to the others and may have dropped it into the mix. Small wonder the prosecutor did not explode.

Janna was lavish in slandering Brenda. But she winced when asked to recognize her father's handwriting in the confession letter. She admitted the writing was similar to his but would not say for certain. She seemed comfortable giving yes or no answers but needed a probe to elaborate.

The prosecution asked about Janna's telephone contact with the fugitives when they were in Mexico. Janna's impression of Brenda exploded in Technicolor. Frustrated by her failure to send them $5,000.00, Brenda had threatened her.

At the FBI's direction, Janna had wired $120.00 to Cancun in late December. On New Years Eve, Brenda had shouted into the phone, "Call and fix the money amount on the check. You little bitch. You need to send me my money."

On cross-examination, Janna sounded happy for her father and Brenda. However she became concerned when he told her about the change in ownership of the insurance policy. It seemed risky for a professional.

Arnett turned bombastic when he questioned Janna about Andrew's asking Pavatt to kill her husband. According to Janna, he had not taken it seriously. He'd related to his daughter, "Andrew...is nuttier than a fruitcake." He told her it was a whim.

Despite Arnett's attempt to discredit her, Janna's testimony about the silver bullet hovered like an elephant in the courtroom. Police ballistics experts testified about the caliber of weapons used to kill Robert Andrew. Common terms in ammunitions description were identified and explained. Words like *stinger, hollow-point,22-long rifle and plinker* elicited detailed description. But the jury panel looked impressed by the clarifications. Both shot-gun shell casings and bullet cartridges were found at the crime scene. The following witness identified additional ammo with connections to the crime.

I felt a catch in my throat when Dean took the stand. He was the State of Oklahoma's 29th witness. The District Attorney wove a careful set of circumstances that made clear that the crime was not the random home invasion purported by the defense. Dean's answers strengthened the state's case for premeditated murder.

When asked about Brenda's growing dislike for her husband, Dean verified that she had stated, "I hate him. I hate him, I hate him," when she talked about Rob. Dean observed that once the divorce proceeded, Brenda's anger intensified.

He pointed out Pavatt when asked to identify the man he'd seen on the Andrew deck, leaning into Brenda with her back against the rail. The tall lean prosecutor placed his hands forward beside Dean, his face positioned close to Dean's nose.

"Is this what you observed on the Andrew's deck, Mr. Gigstad?"

"Yes, sir," replied Dean.

Audience and jurors alike laughed at the theatrics. I chuckled with the rest and was glad for a light moment. My husband looked more relaxed as well.

His testimony continued with the explanation that Brenda and we had exchanged house keys, for cases of emergency. We had mutually agreed to gather papers and mail when one or the other family would vacation. Directed to the murder date, Dean identified a series of photographs taken, various angles showing the proximity of our house and the Andrew home. From these one could see that the distance between our two back doors was but a short span. Easy access to the Andrew deck, hot tub and back door was apparent.

Gieger established that Brenda Andrew had been in our house many times. The succeeding line of questions concentrated on the night we had returned from Kansas, a Sunday night following the murder.

Exhibits #140-144 pictured the bedroom in our house that overlooked the Andrew deck, taken by the forensics team on Monday morning. The bedroom window, with blinds open, gave a clear view of the deck next door,. Exhibit 142, 143 showed the angle from the window opposite the closet door. Dean verified that the closet door had been closed on the date we had left town. Jurors took notes; several eyed the exhibits and paid close attention to Gieger. On the screen, his laser pointer roamed photo surfaces to pinpoint details in the room.

Jurors reacted to the photo of a shotgun shell, sitting upright on its brass end against the open closet door. To a person, they were stunned. The 16-guage shotgun shell sat exactly as we had discovered it that Sunday evening. Someone had hidden inside that bedroom closet. When asked, Dean agreed that no shotgun or weapon was discovered in our house. He further identified 22-guage shells. The forensics team had recovered the shells, strewn across heavy insulation in our attic.

"Do you store your hunting shells in your attic, Mr. Gigstad?" asked Gieger.

"No, I keep them in my bedroom closet," he answered.

The forensics team had been thorough. I recalled the big fellow who had climbed the narrow pull-down stairs into my attic. His stocky build had not been an easy fit. I pictured Pavatt having a much simpler time crawling up.

Finally Dean described the greenbelt behind our property; how easy it would have been for someone to leave our house the morning after the crime. He speculated that a man could have parked his vehicle at an apartment complex less than a fourth-mile from the backyard. Thus, a quick escape.

I inhaled with pride, finally smiled when Dean stepped down from the witness stand. He had recounted exact spaces, time frames and objects as we had discovered them. Detail was his forte.

When forty-four witnesses had testified for the prosecution, Assistant District Attorney Fern Smith announced, "The state proudly rests."

I squirmed when Arnett had his first witness sworn in — our son, Jeff.

Arnett was a short man but nonetheless formidable. He fired questions.

"What about the shooting made you go to your parents' house? What time were you there? Where was the playpen? Was the bedroom closet closed?"

Jeff's responses were unshakeable. He identified photos taken of the spare bedroom, one showing the shotgun shell against the closet door in exhibits # 139 and #145. Arnett tried to discredit Jeff. Unsuccessful, he excused him as witness and called two more. None could exonerate Pavatt.

Lead defense attorney Arnett turned to the judge and stated, "Your honor, the defense rests."

Shock was the only way to describe the look on Judge Susan Bragg's face.

Following a lunch recess, closing arguments preceded jury deliberations.

Prosecutor Gieger reiterated how Pavatt conspired with Brenda to kill Rob Andrew. Touching on Pavatt's braggadocio about his Special Forces career, Gieger said, "He went on one secret mission in his life, when he and Brenda Andrew conspired and killed Rob Andrew. He prophesized and fulfilled his own mission."

Mike Arnett told the jurors that his client made only two mistakes: hooking up with Brenda Andrew and taking her to Mexico. Prosecution's evidence was "purely circumstantial," and the bullet and shotgun shells in our attic could have been easily planted.

I cringed at his implication.

Four weeks had slipped into history when jurors were given instruction and recessed.

CHAPTER 28

Case Rests, Verdict and Sentence

Prosecution and defense attorneys worded their statements to deliver the most impact.

Arnett's plea was, "I know you will do the right thing."

Fern Smith told the jury, "Come back into this courtroom and do justice."

Nine women and three men retired to deliberate Jim Pavatt's culpability in Rob's murder. Two hours and 25 minutes dragged while families, media personnel and witnesses sat with sweaty palms, aching backs and gnawed fingernails. Anxiety made my skin tingle when a door opened and the bailiff led a somber jury back into the room. Judge Bragg received their verdict.

The jury found Pavatt guilty of murder in the 1st degree, and that he was guilty of conspiracy to commit murder. Judge Bragg asked attorneys if they wanted to poll the jury. Prosecutors declined but Arnett accepted. When polled the jury vote was unanimous.

Allowed a recommendation, jurors sentenced Pavatt to ten years, with a $5,000.00 fine on the conspiracy charge. However, they would be required to return the following day to begin the sentencing phase on the murder charge.

Defense attorneys needed time overnight to organize, but prosecutors would have begun sentencing that night.

Meanwhile, reactions to the verdict ran the emotional gamut. James Pavatt sat stone-faced when the verdict was read, mustering a hug for Arnett at the trial's conclusion. Janna Larson unleashed a torrent of tears. Her friend could do little to console her.

Judge Bragg imposed a gag order on the attorneys prior to the sentencing phase. Pain etched on their faces, Pavatt's mother and stepfather refused comment. Opposite them, the Andrew family reacted but did not issue a statement. Rob's youngest brother, Tom had leaned on the bench in front, breathing heavily during his verdict vigil. Attorneys would burn late oil. Neither family would sleep well this night.

By 9:00 A.M. the next day, the two alternate jurors had failed to appear. The panel was finally seated by 10:30 A.M. The prosecution began the case for Pavatt's being given a death sentence. They contended that, by previous threats to his own daughter, Pavatt continued to be a threat to society.

The 911 dispatcher testified that Rob was still conscious during Brenda's call. The medical examiner indicated the victim's wounds to have been painful. Mrs. Smith agreed that the killing was atrocious and cruel, a heinous death.

Silence turned to sniffling sobs when E.R. Andrew took the stand. From a prepared statement, he reminded the court the frustration and pain his family had suffered, from Brenda's insistence that Rob be buried in Oklahoma City rather than Enid to her absence at the funeral service. He spoke of the children's near catatonic state when they returned from Mexico. E.R. halted his testimony for brief periods when he spoke of how Rob had brightened the world for friends and family.

The trauma he and his wife endured had escalated when their grandchildren refused to speak and only chanted, "I want my mommy's family."

Fishing, traveling, biking, hiking and amusement park trips have been a repeated parenting experience for the elder Andrews. Mrs. Smith cried with E.R. during his painful testimony. Jurors wiped salty trickles from taut faces.

Rob's brother Tim lost composure during his statement. A week prior to his death Rob had asked Tim and his wife to keep his children in the event of a catastrophe. Rob had been writing a new will at the time.

Breaking down, Tim said, "Rob will be truly missed; however, we all know he is with the Lord and in a better place."

The Andrew's anguish multiplied with each brother's statement. Bill, the eldest read, "Going through the trial and learning what happened to him is really hard . . . How could anyone do something to someone so gentle?" His eyes glistened, blurring his vision when he looked at the jury,

He continued, "It's tough being the oldest and not having someone to tease, but most of all it hurts to see his children without a father."

Tom Andrew, the youngest sibling, underscored the family's agony by saying, "It's so painful to cry every day and never to sleep at night."

He reminded the audience of Rob's rare sense of humor. He'd sent Tom letters from the family dog, signed with a paw print dipped in ink. Rob would take dozens of photographs on a two-day weekend visit and assemble them into a keepsake album. He'd write letters, assigning each family member a comic strip character.

Tom said, "Rob had such a unique personality that no one could ever replace." When he stepped down, sobs echoed around the room.

Mike Arnett spoke through tears when he addressed the jury. "While you may have found my client guilty of murder, he does not deserve to die." He first questioned Pavatt's mother.

Willie Veteto sympathized with the Andrews and the pain they suffered. Her first husband had been murdered several years past. She maintained that her family was devastated.

Through her tears she said, "My son is a loving person, and if I live to be 100 years old, I will never believe he committed this crime."

I listened to her and tried to feel the meaning of her words. As a mother of sons, I could not put myself in her place. Like Willie, I could not imagine any circumstance that would rattle either of my sons to snap and commit murder. I felt as if we as bystanders, had invaded both families' privacy. Pavatt had catapulted us personally into the fray.

Arnett next called Wade Veteto, Pavatt's stepfather, to speak. Veteto said, "If you have any mercy in your heart, please show it to my son. If you don't, I hope God shows mercy on you." He opened the idea of mercy which the following family and friends would seek.

A cousin, an uncle and a childhood friend clung to the same theory. All described Pavatt as a good man who went to church and loved his family. They contended that he did not deserve to die.

Pavatt's uncle, Chester Veteto, said, "If I had a son, I'd like to have one like him."

Emotion ran high on this day of sentencing. On those seated and waiting I observed tight jaws, tear-streaked faces, sweaty palms and perspiration-soaked clothing. My own feelings surprised me. I felt sorry for Pavatt's family.

In mid-afternoon the attorneys stated their cases for and against Pavatt's receiving the death penalty. Prosecutors based their plea for death on the atrocity of the murder. They made a strong argument for the fact that, though circumstantial, ample evidence existed for the ultimate sentence. Arnett stuck to his contention that no clear finding had implicated his client in a planned execution. The jurors filed to a separate room to begin the deliberating. Both the Andrew and Pavatt families steeled themselves for the outcome.

Five excruciating hours later, the parties filed back into the courtroom. For killing Rob Andrew, the jury recommended that Jim Pavatt should die by lethal injection. Reaction on the Andrew side of the room was a collective gasp.

Janna Larson lay her head in her grandmother's lap and the two cried together. Pavatt turned toward his family, smiled and whispered, "It's okay."

Still smiling, he mouthed, "I love you" to them.

Judge Bragg announced that formal sentencing would happen on October 21, with an automatic appeal allowed.

Interviewed after the sentence was imposed, Assistant District Attorney Fern Smith said, "This was a hard case." Smith spoke matter-of-factly about the trial and results. "There were so many police reports and evidence to put together. We were fortunate to have jurors with common sense who were able to put the puzzle pieces together."

Assistant District Attorney Gayland Gieger voiced similar sentiment and applauded the jurors. "The evidence warranted this decision."

With respect to the Andrew family he continued," We discussed at length the sentencing options, and they understood. They wanted to see justice done, and we did, too."

Conversely, the defense team maintained Pavatt's innocence. "It's not over," said Arnett. "We're quite confident we'll get this reversed on appeal."

Pavatt's family had vacated the courtroom without comment to the media. Arnett stated that they were "very disappointed."

That same evening newscasters and journalists announced Pavatt's sentence. I remained impressed that journalists could assemble the facts, report them with professionalism. Accounts were written with calm detachment rather than emotion.

Following the formal sentencing in October, the Oklahoma Court of Criminal Appeals granted Pavatt an automatic stay of execution. His appeal could be filed and examined.

A confidant Arnett went on the record: "We are very confident of winning the appeal and getting a new trial because of evidence we were not allowed to introduce . . . the outcome will be different."

The prosecuting attorneys differed. Gieger said, "We believe the judge made the correct rulings on the evidentiary issues . . . nothing in the record that will result in a successful appeal."

I pondered their statements and flinched at the possibility of a second trial. Anything was possible, but the Oklahoma Attorney General's office stated that, currently, the average time for appeals might approach seven years, in contrast to a former wait of up to twelve years. We now became players in a new waiting game.

Round two, Brenda's trial, loomed in the near future.

CHAPTER 29

Brenda's Day in Court

Surprise earmarked Brenda Andrew's days in court. The pre-liminary hearing had unlocked the diary of her private life. Her long-anticipated trial would soon become a written record in the Oklahoma County Court records. On May 25, my mail included a subpoena as witness for the State of Oklahoma V. Brenda Andrew. By now I was accustomed to Dean being a witness but was reluctant to categorize myself the same. Nevertheless, I made the necessary arrangements to meet with prosecutors prior to the trial set for June 7, 2004. The prosecution also subpoenaed Dean and Jeff.

I was initially surprised. What could I possibly add to my husband's testimony? Besides, I had committed to writing the story. Would my involvement hinder my observations? Negative thoughts clogged my head. *We* had been victimized and now would *I* be thwarted in my writing endeavor? My daughter-in-law, Sarah, volunteered to attend the trial and take notes. As a witness, I otherwise would be banished from the courtroom.

District Attorney Wes Lane's schedule was clogged. Honor-bound by a political campaign promise to his predecessor, he'd spent time in prosecuting the highly publicized *Terry Nichols* Trial. Nichols was Timothy McVeigh's chief accomplice in the Oklahoma City Murrah Federal Building bombing. Lane's goal, justice for the many victims of that heinous crime, would consume hundreds of man-hours. Consequently, he'd assign an able team from his staff to prosecute Brenda Andrew. Mrs. Fern Smith would act as lead prosecutor. She was accompanied by tall, lanky Gayland Gieger. Prior to her trial, Brenda's attorneys had met with Lane and his staff hoping to plea bargain. They contended that Brenda knew nothing of Pavatt's confession letter and that she had been an unwilling passenger to Mexico.

Lane replied, "I'm not going to buy a pig in a poke..." Brenda's request of immunity seemed ludicrous to the state's case.

Lane's confidence in his team made his physical involvement unnecessary. Later, he stated that "three's a crowd," referring to an old-school legal philosophy about the number of lawyers needed at a courtroom table. He did lament not getting in on the 'fun stuff.'

His showered praises on Fern Smith. "She's the best criminal lawyer west of the Mississippi," he said.

Smith's reputation was impeccable. She had prosecuted over twenty death penalty cases with a perfect conviction record. Together she and Gieger would gather, identify and solidify the evidence, then present a strong case. Mrs. Smith spoke in a quiet controlled voice. Gieger moved across the courtroom, gesturing to make a point. The team presented quiet resolution and minimal theatrics.

Brenda's defense team offered a sharp contrast. Greg McCracken, in early middle-age, had established himself as a crack divorce attorney, hard-nosed in finance tactics. His clients had benefited, and his bankroll had expanded as a result. He presented a notable case to the Oklahoma Supreme Court in 1995 in First Community Bank of Blanchard V. Hodges. McCracken's client won her case versus a bank holding a lien against her ex-husband's property. The court ruled that she recover appeal-related attorney fees. The settlement was a feather in McCracken's cap. He had recently joined the Miskovsky & Miskovsky firm in Oklahoma City.

Although McCracken led, his team included both George Miskovskys II and III. The firm had set public eyes rolling when its founder, Grover Miskovsky, had been convicted of child molestation and racketeering charges. His descendants, now partners in the firm, continued to uphold the notoriety associated with the Miskovsky name. They were known for bombastic court style . McCracken's team compared to the prosecution's like brimstone flame versus icy calm. Having heard from both sides in the Preliminary hearings, I was curious how they would each handle trial witnesses.

The younger attorney, George Miskovsky III, flirted with the law at the end of May, 2004. Complaints were made that he drove a 2002 Mercedes southbound on a major city street with a flat tire. When tested, he was arrested on a drunk-driving charge. I remember reading the newspaper article in awe. Bizarre behavior for a team member on a high-profile murder case, I thought.

Before jury selection could begin, Brenda took the stand before Judge Bragg. Her statements had been taped at police headquarters the night of Rob's death. Prosecutors planned to air its content in court. Andrew's lawyers argued that she should have been *Mirandized* before the interview. But Judge Bragg ruled against them because Andrew had not been considered a suspect at the time. She would allow the tape to be viewed during trial.

Brenda told the judge that she "wants her husband's killers to be found."

McCracken filed for a change of venue. "My client can not receive a fair trial in Oklahoma County because of the extensive media coverage," he stated. The motion was denied.

Delay tactics flourished during the pre-trial month. James Pavatt's confession letter would exonerate Brenda Andrew, her lawyers contended. In addition, information from jail informants about a man who supposedly confessed to the crime was denied. Judge Bragg denied the informant's testimony. McCracken questioned the number of inmates at the Oklahoma County Jail whom prosecutors had interviewed.

Another surprise entered the courtroom in the person of now-convicted killer, James Pavatt. Unlike the tastefully dressed attorneys, Pavatt wore a light-blue button-up shirt and thick-rimmed glasses. In front of the judge, Attorney Arnett asked, "Do you want to assert your Fifth Amendment right not to incriminate yourself?"

Pavatt replied, "Yes."

Assistant District Attorney Fern Smith repeated the same question. She asked him if he knew Brenda's defense had called him as witness.

"I'm exercising my Fifth Amendment," Pavatt replied.

Arnett stated that Pavatt's appeal might be jeopardized if he were to testify at Andrew's trial.

Since Pavatt refused to confirm the contents of his confession letter, the judge must make the final ruling. Pre-trial motions gobbled up days. The paperwork trail threatened to delay the trial events.

Finally, jury selection for Brenda's trial proceeded in the same manner as for Pavatt's. Since June 7, both sides had interviewed potential candidates for the panel. When the number narrowed to thirty, each side could exercise nine challenges, leaving a twelve-member jury. Candidates answered questions about their opinions on the death penalty and pre-trial publicity effects. Seven days of closed-door interviews and open-court procedure resulted in seating the final panel. On June 17, seven men and five women filed into Judge Bragg's court. Polished wooden armchairs with ample legroom between them would suffice for their workplace. Two alternate jurors were selected from a remaining pool of six. The format allowed them to take notes, like in the case of Pavatt's trial.

Local media interviewed attorneys not associated with the case, with their take on the panel. Both suggested that two factors could influence them in Andrew's favor. More men than women may be likely to give an attractive defendant a break. Jurors with jobs dealing with the public may be less sympathetic to a victim. One hundred twenty-five prospects were tapped before the final selection.

More than two years after Rob's death, his wife faced her peers in court. My hand-wringing began as well. Frustrated at not attending the trial, I waited. Sarah took copious notes and described witnesses, jurors, attorneys and defendant in detail. I remained at home until my date in court.

Completing the trial setting were the two detectives who had investigated the case. Detective Roland Garrett and his partner, Gary Damron, would sit at the prosecution's table, opposite Brenda and her attorneys. Garrett had worked for the Oklahoma City Police Department (OCPD) since 1988, promoted to detective in 1997. He had worked in communications for the U.S. Navy prior to his police work. He had worked five homicides prior to the Andrew case. No less qualified, Damron had been a police officer for thirty-six years, investigating homicides for seven years. He'd worked more than 250 case assignments. Both men brought to the table excellent work records, voluminous case loads and extensive experience in crime fighting.

They had not treated Brenda as a suspect the night of the crime but had experienced odd feelings about her from the beginning. Later, Damron would say that "through the interview tapes...we got to see what she's really like." The detectives' testimony during the trial would transfer those "odd" feelings into definite thoughts.

When Judge Bragg entered the court for the opening statements, the static in the air made my skin tingle. A fireworks display on the Fourth of July could not have commanded more tension. Outside the chamber, the elevator doors opened for Brenda to be escorted inside. She cracked a tiny smile for a cameraman trying to snap a candid shot.

A newsman muttered, "We finally got a smile out of her."

Another said, "... She'll be hitting on us all before long."

Jailhouse gossip had Brenda flirting with the bailiffs. An attractive woman, she'd bat her eyelashes at the male escorts, and speak to them in a sweet, small voice with a timid "hi" or "hello." Today she dressed to display a coy, innocent demeanor. But, the conservative dark grey suit, the *grandma appearance*, conflicted with the smug expression on her face when she was seated. False confidence masking fear?.

Opening statements took center stage. Fern Smith quietly stated that the District Attorney was "happy and eager to prove that Brenda Andrew committed both felonies, those of conspiracy to commit murder and first degree murder."

She went on to state that through the witnesses and evidence presented, the State would prove its case against Mrs. Andrew.

McCracken opened the defense with "Mrs. Andrew has long awaited this day too...she's waited two years to prove her innocence." He repeated her long history as an upstanding *Lutheran*, both in church and college. At least one audience member's eyes glazed from *Lutheran's* overuse. McCracken painted Brenda's as an exemplary bank employee (once named Employee of the Year), and Rob's own journal entry of her superb ability as mother and the spiritual leader of their family.

Brenda glowed during his elaborate word picture of her accomplishments. Easy to see how McCracken's prowess shone in divorce court. Stating that friends and neighbors (we Gigstads included) had trusted Brenda and had accompanied her to her divorce hearing as character witnesses, he expounded on the friendship angle with gusto. Referring to the crime, he pointed out the brightly-lit Andrew household, popping noises the neighbors heard and Brenda's loyalty to her friends. She had been diligent with a call to the Gigstads in Kansas to tell them about Rob's death. (Later, during my testimony, he was shown to be wrong on this count, a minor detail.)

When McCracken concluded his opening statement, Judge Bragg reminded the jury, "You will determine what the evidence proves."

— — — — — — — — — — — — — — — — — — — —

Trial format specified that first the prosecution, then the defense, would present their cases, calling multiple witnesses to the stand. Each could be cross-examined by the opposite side. Final arguments would then precede the evidence going to jury for deliberation. Mountains of paper evidence had been wheeled into the room. Prosecution called its first witness, Mark Sinor.

Pastor Sinor served North Pointe Baptist Church at the time of the Andrews' divorce hearings, during the time when Rob's brake lines had been cut, and at the trial date. When Rob had confided in him, he warned Rob not to approach his wife.

"I have no doubt that Rob Andrew feared for his life," he said.

He had counseled with Brenda at an earlier date and concluded that "she could care less about Rob."

The next witness, Pastor Michael Fetters had served at North Pointe until the summer of 2001, knowing both the Andrews. He stated, "Rob was really hurting. He was saddened and afraid at the same time." When cross-examined for proof that Brenda killed Rob, he repeated that Rob's concerns for his life were very real.

The state planned on calling nearly forty witnesses and the scenes were being set. When Stanley Morgan took the stand, the audience perked up. Morgan had testified in the preliminary hearing, admitting to a three-year affair and friendship with Brenda. Oddly, Morgan said that he and Brenda had remained friends long after their sexual desires waned. Although he denied that Brenda asked him to kill Rob, he did say that she said on numerous occasions that she hated her husband. Worried about being named Rob's life insurance policy beneficiary, she'd been upset. Matter-of-fact now, Morgan's role as paramour appeared as a proof of Brenda's infidelity. McCracken's cross-examination hammered home the fact that Morgan knew nothing abut a murder plot.

Like Morgan, witness Rick Nunley spoke about his friendship with Brenda. When asked about previous questioning at the preliminary hearing, Nunley suffered a convenient memory lapse.

He said, "I can't remember my previous testimony about Brenda Andrew and all this."

When pressed, he admitted to visiting her once in jail, having limited contact. McCracken asked him to describe Brenda as a person. Enthusiastic, he portrayed her as "intelligent, a nice person, a good mom and *very hospitable.*"

Despite Brenda's ability to endear good friends, she affected others in peculiar ways. David Ostrowe had met her in September, 2001 at a dinner meeting with Rob. A self-described headhunter, Ostrowe and Associates helped Rob with staffing needs at Jordan Associates. The two had become friends and thought their wives would find common interests. At Rob's invitation, Ostrowe and his wife waited at a local restaurant. Knowing Rob's conservative beliefs, Ostrowe expected a woman with a similar view.

"Who's the hoochie?" Initial reaction to Brenda prompted his wife's side comment.

Ostrowe continued, "Brenda wore a slinky tight dress, heavy on the cleavage. Her hairstyle was dark and gothic. She talked a lot about how much she loved Mexico, how beautiful the beaches are."

He described the dinner conversation as being entirely weird. "She talked about how the workmen on her deck would baby sit her kids while Rob was at work, how she loved them because they helped her a lot."

Finally, he said, "The pleasantries aside, we couldn't exit the place fast enough."

Rob's idea of a friendly foursome had come to an abrupt halt.

Another witness, college student Jennifer Jones, had known Brenda much longer, since 1998-99. Jones worked odd jobs to help pay tuition expenses. She testified that she had worked as a nanny, taking children in her care to *Dynamo* gymnastics studio. In the gallery of waiting mothers she had met Brenda. While waiting for classes to end, one day Brenda pulled her aside to chat. Right off, Jennifer noticed Brenda's wedding ring.

"I complimented her on the large stone," she said. "Instead of accepting the compliment, Brenda told me about her good friend, Rick Nunley, getting a divorce. His wife, Cindy, was one of the gymnastics mothers. Brenda said she had spent a lot of time with Rick lately and it bothered Rob a lot."

Jennifer continued, "I thought the look on her face was more delighted than concerned. Brenda was afraid Cindy Nunley might harm her. That's why she took me downstairs to talk. But Mrs. Nunley didn't bother her. Brenda asked me to come over to watch her son.

"She called me two days ahead to baby sit while she ran errands and bought groceries. When I got there Brenda was dressed in all leather clothes and had her hair fixed *really big,* much different than what she wore to *Dynamo.*"

Miss Jones related that Brenda said, "Stay in Connor's room or the kitchen. Don't go in any other rooms. Don't answer the phone or the door." However, Jones did walk by and glance into the living room. Two couches were placed back-to-back. She thought it odd. The time couldn't pass fast enough for her.

Jones said, "When Brenda returned, she had no groceries and her hair was all messed up. She wore no wedding ring. I asked her where it was."

Brenda had replied, "I took the car to *Red Carpet* for washing and put the ring in the ash tray. Sometimes it is so big and heavy on me. When they washed the car, those bastards took my ring."

Prosecutors asked Jones about the second time she babysat for Brenda.

"She called at the last minute," Jones said. "She gave me the same instructions as before, about what rooms I could go in, no doorbell or phone. Brenda was dressed in a provocative outfit, the same as before. When she got home, she had no groceries."

"She called me again and left messages on my answering machine. I called her back, no answer, and left the message that I couldn't babysit."

Asked to continue, Jones related, "Rob Andrew called my number, said he had gotten my message. He wanted to know *who* I was, *why* had I been at his house and *how many times* I had been there."

She detected emotion, real concern in his voice. At that point she decided never to return to the Andrew home.

After her testimony, I could make sense of my own experience with Jones. On Brenda's recommendation, I had hired her to clean my house a few times. I had thought it odd that she parked a good block away from our house. She had given me notice after three times. Her class schedule had changed. Later, I had learned the truth.

Jones told me, "I didn't want Brenda to see my car at your house and pressure me to baby sit. One day I saw her leaning into the window of a turquoise car in her driveway. The man in the car had a mustache. I had a feeling something was going on and I didn't want any part of it."

So much for Brenda's reputation. I wondered what effect these early testimonies were having on the jurors.

Reputation, motive for murder, physical evidence, emotional responses –the puzzle pieces began to fit as the trial wore on.

CHAPTER 30

Puzzle Pieces Fit Together

At its midpoint, no new surprises splashed into the trial scene. Witnesses became comfortable answering questions asked by both sides. Ronnie Stump's experience stemmed from the preliminary hearing, a trial in Enid regarding the Andrew children's custody and Pavatt's trial.

Emphasis now concentrated on multiple phone calls and letters exchanged between him and Rob Andrew during the divorce ordeal. Four taped telephone calls demonstrated Rob's concerns. In them, Brenda had accused her husband of having an affair with a work-place friend, calling the woman "slut" and "bitch." She accused Rob of dating before his divorce was final. Ronnie's emotions gagged him when he was asked to read the contents of a letter. He choked, sobbed and handed the paper to prosecutors to read. Rob had asked him " . . . to pray for him, the kids, Brenda and (this is a hard one, but) Jim too."

Of later importance was a statement from Rob on November 19, 2001. "You'll be glad to know Brenda doesn't think I'm having an affair with a woman anymore – now she thinks I'm gay, with you."

On cross-examination, McCracken blasted Stump. He accused Ron of making up the *gay* testimony, an attempt to smear Brenda's character.

Stump lost his composure a second time when Smith asked him to describe his feelings when he learned Rob had been killed.

"I turned to my wife and I said '(They)...killed him.' "

Smith asked, "Who were you referring to?"

Stump answered, "Brenda Andrew and James Pavatt."

McCracken hammered Stump with queries about his having proof that Brenda planned to kill her husband. Smith often objected with "asked and answered." The judge ruled to sustain her objections.

Barbara Murcer Green had known Rob Andrew for fourteen years, most recently at Jordan Associates. She spoke about the incident when Brenda had burst into a meeting at the office and had begun the fight with Rob.

"Rob was humiliated," she said.

She observed Brenda taking items from Rob's office after he had left. Green asked Brenda to leave or she would call the police.

Brenda walked up to her, bumped her with her belly and said, "Call them. And you'd better watch your back."

McCracken cross-examined her about Brenda's threats to kill Rob.

Green replied, "Yes, on the speakerphone in Rob's office prior to the divorce hearing. Rob told her he was going to file for joint custody and Brenda told she'd 'see him dead.'"

Roger Frost, Lansbrook Security officer and an Oklahoma City Police Officer as well, took the stand. He had been the first officer at the crime scene. He had driven Brenda to Baptist Hospital for treatment of the gunshot wound to her arm. He described the spectacle in the Andrew garage and verified a picture on the courtroom monitor with Rob's blood-soaked body lying on the floor.

A glance at Brenda brought no reaction. She stared at the image and did not look away, showing no feeling.

Frost verified that he had seen a tremendous amount of gunshot residue on Brenda's arm, as if the gun had nearly touched her. George Miskovsky III showed pictures of Brenda's wound being treated. He tried to get Frost to agree that Brenda had been in shock, explaining her lack of emotion. Frost did not waiver, still saying that Brenda was 'calm and unemotional' when he took her to a friend's house.

Gieger re-directed the questioning, pulling the photo of Brenda's face, flinching in pain in the hospital bed and replacing it with the one of Rob dead in the garage. At this point, Rob's mother turned away from the stark images, a trying moment. But Brenda looked at the picture without blinking.

A back-and-forth display of contrasting photos turned into a power struggle between opposing counsels. On cross, Miskovsky replaced Rob's image with Brenda's. Mrs. Smith reached up while he was talking and plucked his picture off the monitor. Miskovsky paused for a second or two, stunned.

The state's next witness was Officer Teresa Bunn. She had met Brenda in the hospital. She'd asked the patient about a bruise on her right leg.

Brenda had replied, "I got it roller-skating with the kids and Rob, trying to patch things up the Friday before Rob's death."

Bunn said, "Brenda never asked me to check on Rob. She asked repeatedly about her kids."

Bunn further supported Frost's testimony about a lack of blood trail into the house. She had not seen any such trail nearby or on a phone cradle, either from the garage or into the master bedroom. She identified a card admitted into evidence, from Brenda to James, signed *Love, Brenda*. A flashlight, turned on but with a dead battery, and Rob's wallet containing $65.00 in cash were items Bunn had recovered from the garage. Odd for would-be robbers to neglect a bulging billfold.

On cross-examination, the defense belittled Bunn's credentials. They implied that investigators may form pre-conceived ideas about a person at the crime scene as to guilt or innocence. Again, condescension ruled their questions. Bunn responded to one, stating that while in the army for nineteen years, she had dealt with people in shock.

Miskovsky's voice blared, his random gesturing extreme . He dipped his hand into an evidence bag, grabbed Brenda's pink sweater from it and asked, "Is that all the blood from her wound on that shirt?" He waved the garment in front of the jurors, closing in on them.

Judge Bragg ordered him, "Get back from the jury with that. Quit waving that thing all around."

Continuing, Miskovsky pursued the fact that no blood trail was found in the house. When his tone escalated to a roar, the judge told him to "stop doing that. Just stop that right now."

The following series of testimonies came from Oklahoma City Police officers Klicka, Niles, the service manager who had replaced Rob's cut brake lines, the plumber who had argued with Brenda about payment and a friend from Wiley Post School. Each verified statements made in earlier testimony from the preliminary hearing or from Pavatt's trial. Plumber David Head injected no new evidence but provided a light moment in the somber events.

McCracken asked, "Are you presently incarcerated at the Oklahoma County Jail?"

Head answered, "No, I'm presently at the Oklahoma County courthouse." Ripples of laughter in the room followed his remark.

Three weeks before Rob's murder, his associate Rod Lott observed an unusual reaction from Rob about Brenda. The graphic designer at Jordan had met Rob for lunch. Rob said he was worried about the marriage, that Brenda said she wished him dead. She'd changed the locks on the house doors and wouldn't let him collect his clothes or his shotgun.

Lott had known Rob for thirteen years, had traveled with him on business trips. Returning from Tulsa, he heard Brenda's voice on Rob's speakerphone in the car. The conversation was dry, cut off with no endearment. Lott had asked, "Why do you not tell her 'I love you,' on the phone?"

Rob had answered, "Early on, Brenda told me that saying that made her uncomfortable and to not say it anymore."

Rob had confided to Lott about Brenda's friendship with Rick Nunley. He'd found Rick at their house and asked Brenda about it. She'd call him 'silly.' Rob said that he'd followed her to Rick's house once. She'd parked her car in Nunley's garage. Rob had gone to the front door, rang the bell but got no answer.

Lott said further that Rob confided that he and Brenda had not had sex in years. On occasion, he'd come home to find she'd purchased new lingerie. He was badly hurt that he never got to see her wear the sexy pieces.

Lott's testimony revealed the inner emotions of a severely bruised marriage., especially Rob Andrew's battered ego.

Following an attempt to disallow the defense's handwriting analyst to testify, the judge ruled to allow it. Both she and David

Parrett, the handwriting analysis expert for the state, injected no new evidence about the documents they examined than from previous exposures in court. Pavatt's confession letter was admitted into evidence after nearly an hour of up-close conference with the judge.

Parrett stated, "You can only write *worse* than you normally do, but you cannot write any *better* than your normal skill level." Defense attorneys tried to discredit his remark.

Miskovsky grilled Parrett. "This letter is not to be taken lightly, is it? It was an integral part in the prosecution of James Pavatt." Parrett gave no answer, over objections. The defense continued, "This letter exonerates Brenda Andrew, doesn't it?"

Again, over objections, Parrett did not answer. Brenda's defense had raised a legitimate question.

Bill Andrew affirmed that Rob owned a 16-guage single shot shotgun. Rob had told him he was excited to go quail hunting with his brothers over Thanksgiving. However, he was worried that Brenda wouldn't give him his shotgun. For both sides, Bill explained how that particular gun worked, a break-open barrel.

Detective Roland Garrett was next to answer. He had talked with Brenda in the hospital, inviting her to be interviewed at police headquarters downtown. She was willing. While waiting for the detectives, she sat in the conference room, slouched and messing with her hair. On camera, she held her arm and fiddled with her bandage when Garrett entered. Covered by two hospital gowns, Brenda voluntarily answered questions for more than two hours.

When Garrett told her that her husband was dead she had a blank look on her face. She said, "But he was breathing." She never shed a tear.

Garrett questioned her about her love, or lack of it, for Rob. She said she "hated him because he said mean things to me."

Garrett had asked, "Did you ever have any extramarital affairs?"

"No — never," she replied. Brenda seemed more interested in seeing her kids than hearing about her dead husband.

While Garrett talked, Brenda watched the monitor in the courtroom, her face void of expression.

Back in the interview, Garrett had asked her if anyone she knew would have wanted Rob dead. He asked specifically if James Pavatt would have been out to get Rob.

Brenda had been emphatic. "*No*, James Pavatt wouldn't even benefit from it. James Pavatt was only a financial advisor."

She denied seeing what happened after shots were fired and where the intruders might have gone. Her main worries concerned the time she could go back into her house and get her purse and credit cards, asking him three or four times.

Prosecutors asked Garrett what items he had discovered, both in the Andrew home on Shaftsbury and in belongings recovered from the Mexico trip. In the house the detectives found credit card receipts, mortgage coupons and a paper copy of a plane ticket to Korea for Sukui Pavatt (paid by Brenda's Visa card). From Pavatt's belongings and the luggage, they recovered a Visa to enter Mexico (destination, Monterrey coast), copies of birth certificates and a form allowing Pavatt to drive a car across the border. His current credit card statements indicated Pavatt had been heavily in debt.

Gieger had entered into evidence six large pieces of luggage, three smaller bags, a black backpack and a large box holding miscellaneous small items. An item of interest was an Agatha Christie novel titled, *Murder Is Easy*. Alongside it was a handwritten note titled, *book report on Agatha Christie book*.

Cross-examination became a lengthy discourse by the defense. Miskovsky attempted to bring Pavatt's confession into his speech, implying that Pavatt had been irate over a possible Andrew reconciliation and had acted alone. The judge continued to sustain prosecutors' objections.

Miskovsky introduced the Agatha Christie book as possibly the only one Brenda could find in Mexico, suitable for Genesee's book report. He implied that Brenda acted in good faith, being a good mother, seeking agreement from Garrett.

It became a contest of semantics.

Miskovsky was indignant. "What? An Agatha Christie book — it's some pornographic book or something."

Garret replied, "No — but it's not an appropriate book for a nine-year old to be reading."

"Why? And that's just your opinion, right? Why?"

"Because of the title first of all, *Murder Is Easy*," stated Garrett.

The party's last balloon popped when Miskovsky badgered Garrett about the arrest warrant for the fugitives. He belabored each paragraph of the document, arguing the legality of a free America citizen leaving the country for a vacation. His voice boomed like thunder when Fern Smith nearly had to scream "*Objection!*" to be heard. Judge Bragg mercifully stepped in.

"Stop! You are badgering the witness and it is completely unprofessional! I won't allow that!"

From police procedures, the trial path turned to the Enid minister who had officiated at Rob's funeral service. Wade Burleson had come to the Andrew home at Brenda's request. She, her mother and her kids had been present. But Burleson talked to Brenda aside. Not knowing Rob, he had asked, "Can you tell me what it is that you will miss about your loved one who has died?"

The minister related that Brenda had stared at him, with no response. He repeated the question, asking for a possible story or anecdote he might relate to mourners at the service.

Brenda replied, "Nothing."

Burleson testified, "In twenty-five years of doing this, I have never had that response. It was awkward, no care or concern at all."

On cross-examination, McCracken implied that Burleson painted a negative picture of Brenda because of his friendship with Rob's parents. When he said, "I know you don't like Brenda," the judge raised her voice.

"Stop," she said. "Approach now!"

Her stern face disclosed nothing while she talked to him. But when McCracken walked away from the bench, she admonished him. "Stay right here. We're not done yet." She had reprimanded Miskovsky but this was her first for McCracken. Impassioned pleas become the norm when a defendant's life is at stake.

A ninety-year-old farmer, Herman Roggow, took the stand. He had to walk to the table where Brenda sat to identify her before the court. Knowing her father and grandfather, he pointed her out as the passenger in a car he had seen within view of a canyon bordering his land. Locals knew it as a place to target-shoot. Roggow had seen its occupants unloading guns from the car. Exhibiting her first sentiments, Brenda cried when the old man stood before her at the trial.

Subsequent witnesses included a man from whom Pavatt wanted to buy a 22-caliber gun, the police officer who interviewed him, the owner of a gun shop where Pavatt *did* buy the 22-caliber gun, a *Plinker,* Jeff Gigstad indicating the time frame when he was in our house, Dean Gigstad talking about a hot tub conversation with Brenda and finally, the two policemen telling abut evidence at our house. No prints had been lifted, but 22-caliber shells were scattered across the attic insulation.

Pavatt's daughter, Janna Larson, was on the stand less than an hour. She painted negative images of Brenda, her father's lover. In October, 2001 Pavatt told Janna that Brenda had asked him to kill Rob or if he knew someone who would. Janna said that her father had referred to Brenda as *"nuttier than a fruitcake."*

On cross, McCracken hammered the fact that it had been Pavatt, not Brenda, who had said incriminating things about a murder.

Kurt Stoner, an FBI Special Agent, told about giving Janna a cell phone to track phone calls between her and the fugitives if they contacted her from Cancun, Mexico. Earlier, the authorities had missed tracking the exact location by about an hour.

Nearing the final expected witnesses for the prosecution, tension showed on the spectators' faces.

Police Detective Gary Damron, Garrett's partner talked about an audio tape entered into evidence. The phone call between Rob and Brenda took place on November 17, 2001, days before the crime. The children spent the evening with Rob, as part of the temporary divorce settlement. Brenda's hysterics ran rampant throughout the call. Attempting to talk her daughter into wanting to leave Rob's apartment, she told Genesee to "be strong, to stand up for herself." The talk switched to Connor's dog, Pepper.

Brenda had asked her son, "Did Pepper pee on Rob's carpet today?"

Connor replied, "No but he pooped on the carpet."

Brenda's response was, "Yea! Good job, Pepper!" She asked him if it stunk.

Rob was definitely being made out as "the bad guy." Brenda assured Genesee that she was figuring things out so they wouldn't have to stay with Rob again.

The prosecution's 50th witness was sworn in. Gordon Robertson, a firearms examiner, was Senior Criminalist for the Oklahoma State Board of Investigation (OSBI). He had determined that the 16-guage shotgun shells found in the garage were fired from the same shotgun. A 22-guage round taken from the Andrew garage/house door was the same type as the bullet taken from Janna Larson's car. Smith asked him to confirm what a shot intended to do the least amount of damage would do to the outside of an arm, exactly like Brenda's wound.

Pieces came together in a tighter fit with the state's 51st witness, Tom Bevel. A forensics professor specializing in crime scene reconstruction, he concluded that Brenda had stood in front of the door leading from the garage to the house when she was shot. He testified that the first shotgun blast had wounded Rob when he was squatting 3-14 feet away. The second shot, in the neck, was from much closer range than the first, from four feet or closer.

Bevel stated that the Brenda's phone had no blood on it. In addition, no blood was found anywhere in the house. The blood spatter pattern indicated that Brenda was not shot by any of the pellets that struck Rob.

Cross-examination tried to intimidate the police work at the crime scene, implying possible tampering with the phone. Brenda, they said, had blood on her hands when photographed in the hospital.

Smith re-directed Bevel's statement to conclude that "all blood on Brenda's jeans was DNA tested and ruled as *female* blood."

"At this time your Honor, the State proudly rests," stated Mrs. Smith.

CHAPTER 31

Defense Responds, the Outcome

Long-anticipated, Brenda's defense primed for the fight. July 8, 2001 McCracken called his first witness, Richard Hull, a heating and air service contractor. Hull said that the Andrew garage furnace unit had a crack in the heat exchange, a reason for the pilot light blowing out. On cross-examination, he denied knowing of a second unit in the house.

Next-door neighbors to the east testified about the fight between Brenda and plumber, David Head, confirming their concern for Brenda's safety. The neighbor's wife talked about the night of the crime. She reported that Brenda had been a kind neighbor, often baking desserts for them.

James Ramsey, police officer at the crime scene, said that he moved Brenda from near Rob's body to a doorstep about two feet away. From his experience, he determined that Rob was deceased. He had gone to the master bedroom where the kids were watching television and asked if they had heard anything. According to him, they both shrugged. Smith did not cross-examine him.

After an OKC paramedic had re-affirmed Brenda's extreme anxiety over her kids and their welfare, a funeral director from Vondel L. Smith Mortuary testified. Ms. Kimmel said that Brenda was quiet and subdued while picking out a casket. She paid in full for the funeral expenses. The following day she brought her children with her, taking them to the room where Rob lay in his casket and closed the door. Again, limited cross-examination.

A County Jail inmate testified that Brenda had been shy and wouldn't talk to anyone there. She said that inmates had access to news accounts in the Andrew case. The girl said that the inmate who had testified for the prosecution was known as a "jailhouse snitch." Smith disagreed, saying, "Are you aware this is the first case T. Sullivan has ever testified in?"

Defense attorneys called their tenth witness, an expert criminal investigator with twenty-nine years experience. Gieger questioned Ron Gardner's credibility as an expert, his having worked but one homicide, with two cold cases in four years. He had testified in two cases (of 70 worked) for trajectory, admitting that he disliked the math portion of such analyses. Judge Bragg certified Gardner in crime scene reconstruction and blood stain analysis but not in trajectory. His primary trial experience had been as a defense witness.

Defenders prodded the judge to certify him in trajectory investigation. Judge Bragg smothered the effort three times. Lengthy credential lists, multiple courses passed in criminology and blood stain analysis fell short in qualifying his expertise in determining trajectory. Finally, facing the jury and prosecutors, Gardner started a Power Point presentation.

His screen displayed three important blood patterns on Brenda's jeans. The first showed a spatter, not a drip. The second was a spatter. Gardner was never confident about the identity of the third stain, an odd pattern. Because her shirt soaked up a significant amount of blood, he said that Brenda had not been dripping blood at the scene.

Gardner fidgeted when Gieger objected to statements he made. The prosecutor's objection was sustained.

He continued his testimony saying, "Brenda was three feet from the door when she was shot, according to the projectile found in the door. There is no evidence of crime scene staging, but of event staging. "

He believed that every aspect of Brenda's statements in the police interview was consistent with findings at the crime scene.

Gieger implied in his cross that Gardner based his assumption about the door being closed, in agreement with Brenda's story and statements. Gieger asked him about the possibility that the shooter was involved with the staging. He asked Gardner, "Is it *possible* Brenda Andrew was also involved in this staging?"

Gardner replied, "I can't rule that out. It's definitely *not* a random shooting."

He readily confirmed that all his expenses were covered by the defense team. He denied having access to the OCPD's testing facility. He had not done DNA testing on Brenda's bloody jeans. The witness answered in short, snippy defensive terms. He did verify that Tom Bevel, the prosecution's expert witness, was his respected mentor.

Gieger continued, "Is it possible Brenda Andrew did not go into the house?"

"I can't rule that out – I don't know where she went or didn't go," Gardner answered.

"Do you think Brenda's shirt soaked up all her blood from the wound?"

"No," he replied. "I don't think that or would expect that it would."

Another contradiction occurred in reference to Rob's body positioning when he was shot. Gardner placed Brenda on Rob's right side during the second shot, when she got *no* blood spatter. His analysis put Brenda at the back door when she was wounded, precisely the time Rob took the second blast.

Gieger's final jab at Gardner must have been embarrassing. "Do you have a clue why Mr. McCracken didn't test any of the blood at your request?"

"No," was the reply.

After a brief recess for arguments of law to be handled, Judge Bragg announced that the defense had rested its case. Closing arguments resumed the following Monday.

— — — — — — — — — — — — — — — — — — —

Attorney Fern Smith was first to speak for the State of Oklahoma. She thanked jurors for their time and attentiveness. She stated that, at the border crossing, no evidence proved that Andrew was turning herself in to authorities. The evidence showed the pair were *broke*, needed money. As of November 19, there was no evidence of reconciliation between Brenda and Rob. Rob's computer log showed, "Brenda called me, told me to 'Go to hell' and hung up."

About Pavatt moving his washer and dryer into the Andrew house, Smith asked, "Does that sound like James Pavatt thought Brenda was going to reconcile with Rob?"

Smith went on to state the requirements for a Murder I conviction: death of a human, an unlawful death, death caused by the defendant, death caused by malice and forethought. The elements necessary to prove conspiracy to commit murder are: agreement, to commit the crime with malice and forethought, the defendant a party to the agreement and an overt act by one or more of the parties performed subsequent to the agreement.

She showed that Pavatt's confession letter was full of Brenda's words, like "you didn't love your dad..."

She concluded with readings from Rob's ideal marriage list. In the courtroom, overt crying shattered silences. Smith spoke for one and a half hours.

In sharp contrast, Greg McCracken closed for the defense, talking for nearly three and a half hours. He began, "Brenda Andrew does not have to prove she is innocent. The state has to prove beyond reasonable doubt that she is guilty. Why is the burden so great? Because Brenda's personal freedom is at stake."

McCracken called the State's case a *boogie bear* attempt to discredit his client. He thrust at the jury the fact that no witness had seen or heard of Brenda having a plot to kill Rob. He insisted that Pavatt had fallen in love with Brenda and had acted alone. He also said, as her divorce lawyer, that the Andrews were not getting a divorce. "They were just in their up and down cycle."

When he read Pavatt's confession letter, he stressed the words *I, me, my* in the document. Harping on *reasonable doubt,* he asked the jury to be impartial. McCracken mentioned the state's witnesses who had performed a character assassination on Brenda. Even Rob's diary entries had not called Brenda *mean.*

McCracken called the life insurance policy a *red herring,* not a motive for murder. He played down Parret's analysis of the forged insurance documents. The more he belittled the state's evidence, the louder and more theatric his voice became. A reminder of Pavatt's guilt, he flapped the confession letter in the air.

Repeating that *circumstantial evidence* is the lynchpin of the prosecution's case, McCracken was adamant that no case had been proved.

"This case reeks with reasonable doubt and the only verdict you can find is *not guilty*," he finished.

Gieger finalized closing for the prosecution. "This room *reeks* of the guilt of Brenda Andrew. Rob Andrew speaks to us from his grave," he said. "My grandfather told me that people yell when they run out of things to say."

After playing the 911 tape, Gieger reminded the jury that witness statements under oath cannot be twisted. Nor can AT&T phone records or taped calls be twisted. He reminded the court about signature dates on the insurance policy; the fact that Rob was in Las Vegas on business during the exact time and date he had supposedly signed it.

Gieger played taped phone conversations and the 911 call from Rob's apartment. "You can't twist the facts about events and how Brenda changed her story."

He continued, "the police interview tape reinforced her lack of interest in Rob's welfare. Instead, she *did* ask to go home, not common sense."

When he reconstructed the crime scene, Gieger made clear that DNA blood testing of the spatters on her jeans implicated her. "The #5 back-spatter is conclusive that Brenda fired the assassination shot, the second shot. There was no blood on the bag of cans nearby."

Gieger went on, "The evidence shows where she went to be shot. Why would James Pavatt shoot her unless the act was staged? Shooting her draws attention to him, not her." He pulled an exhibit from the luggage, a black and red negligee, thong underwear and bathing suits. When she ran to Mexico, Gieger stressed that her behavior was a weird way of showing grief.

As for the confession letter, Gieger stated, "The state never believed the letter as anything more than a concoction. What kind of freak would write that to a ten-year old child?"

He played the earlier tape, from Rob's apartment. Referring back to the letter he said, "whose words do those sound like?"

He read from Rob's journal about Brenda's infidelity, also

played his conversation with Stump stating," I think she finally found someone to kill me." Gieger rested his case.

The jury retired to deliberate.

Monday afternoon, at 3:50 p.m. Judge Bragg received the verdict. *Guilty* on both counts: Murder 1 and Conspiracy to commit murder. Jurors suggested to the court an arbitrary 10-year sentence on the murder count and a $5,000.00 fine for the conspiracy conviction.

The penalty phase would take place Wednesday morning at 9:00 a.m. Witnesses would appear for both sides.

When verdict and sentence were read, Brenda shed no tears. Stoic, she turned to her attorney and followed him from the room. Tension permeated the courtroom because justice might yet be served in the penalty phase to come.

CHAPTER 32

Two and a Half Years Later, Penalty

July 14, 2004 was a typical steamy Oklahoma day. Inside Judge Bragg's courtroom, suspense ruled. Brenda Andrew's fate would be decided by the jurors who had found her guilty of murder two days before. Assistant District Attorney Fern Smith opened for the prosecution. Matter-of-factly, she stated the Bill of Particulars for seeking the death penalty.

Rob's murder had been accomplished for remuneration, the proceeds of the $800,000.00 life insurance policy. Photographs indicated the crime had been cruel and heinous. The defendant would continue to be a threat in society.

Smith contended that from late October of 2001, Rob had felt threatened by his wife and her lover, citing the cut brake lines. Especially heinous, the victim had still been alive at the time Brenda's 911 call was taped. Finally, Smith said, "Brenda Andrew valued money. She took her kids to Mexico. Do justice for the State of Oklahoma, with the death penalty."

George Miskovksy III opened the morning for the defense. Sensitive, sympathetic, he spoke so softly to the jury that those in the gallery could barely hear him. Re-enforcing Brenda's education, love for family and children, neighborliness, record as a good employee and her Christianity, he concluded, "Come let us reason together."

The witness parade had an orderly but highly charged effect on those present. Rob Andrew's father, E.R. Andrew, led the procession with his victim impact statement, relating events from his initial reaction at his son's death to the overflow crowd attending Rob's funeral, his words choked with emotion. This *grandfather-now- parent* related the severe trauma that the Andrew children had to bear, and his role in parenting a second family.

Rob's brothers testified about their great loss, how vacant life felt without him. Most important, all three stressed the void Rob's children would feel without his sunny personality. Following few questions on cross-examination, the state rested.

Paul Southwick, Brenda's first cousin, spoke in her favor. "She's a precious flower, a beautiful person," he said. He related family childhood memories with the Evers siblings. When Southwick talked about Brenda's steadfast commitment to her mentally challenged brother, Brenda wiped her eyes. Her tears flowed while he exalted her as a *good mom*. Southwick saw her life still with purpose, being a witness and teacher to inmates.

Aunt Marilyn Evers called Brenda "the glue that held the family together when Don (Brenda's father) died." Brenda's letters had cheered her up when her own husband had died recently. Her plea for her niece was, "She is a worthy, wonderful person. Preserve her life. She could come in contact with someone you love."

I was glued to my seat during these testimonials. Compassion for my former friend compelled me to agree with their heart-wrenching bequests. But reality jolted me back to earth when a psychologist for the defense got on the stand. Terese Hall was certified as an expert witness. She had interviewed Brenda for up to seven hours prior to the trial. She concluded that Brenda possessed extremely low risk factors. Based solely on her interview, without knowledge of the actual case facts, she declared Brenda competent.

By noon, we all felt the weight of our mixed feelings. Both families had undergone undeniable anguish, apparent in their gut-wounding words. I doubted that any would enjoy the lunch break.

Kim Bowlin, Brenda's sister, tweaked our guilt with stories of their handicapped brother. Kim said, "He doesn't understand why she's gone." Brenda's face was streaked with tears while her sister spoke.

Bowlin's fifteen-year old daughter testified, saying that Brenda had always been there for her. She let loose a tearful torrent while being questioned.

Lutheran pastor, Reverend Joseph Myers had talked to Brenda about all the loss in her life. He was impressed that she currently was studying the Bible.

"Brenda Andrew has a great love for people," he said. "Life is meaningful, even in the most restrictive manner."

His witness became a narrative on the death penalty and how wrong he believed it. In reply, Gieger asked him if he thought Rob received mercy.

The defense called, as it tenth witness, Genesee Andrew. The child drowned in tears and could not read either of two letters she'd written to her mother. McCracken read them for her. Several jurors cried openly during the spectacle. Gieger simply asked her if they had been written a long time ago. She nodded her head 'yes.' Later, in the newspaper, an unrelated Oklahoma attorney penned a letter to the editor sharply criticizing the defense attorneys. He labeled using the child as a witness *shameful*.

Rose Evers painted a beautiful picture of her daughter. Two jurors cried when Rose described the special bond between them as only a mother and child can share. Her final plea was," I beg you jurors. But she is my child and I beg of you to let her live."

When the defense rested, late in the afternoon, the judge gave instructions.

Smith offered the state's first closing remarks. She said, "The death penalty should be Brenda Andrew's reward for what she has earned. She deserves the same sympathy she showed Rob – when she murdered him in their garage. ...we don't ask you to do the hard thing or easy thing...we ask you to do the *right* thing."

McCracken stated his plea quietly, in opposition to his earlier demeanor in front of jurors. He talked about the Andrew children, "how they should get to touch, hold, hug, have their mother as they grow up....no eye witness saw the shooting. You have alternatives that you can give. What would Rob say?"

He continued, "The children need to deal with it and her some day. I ask you to give her life. Choose life in prison. She could do good in the future."

McCracken's cohort, Miskovsky, took the floor. His forte was drama. Pointing at jurors, raising his voice, he quoted Thomas Jefferson once and accused the prosecution of using 'word craft' with manipulating the instructions to the jury. Copying Gieger, he asked, "What does your common sense tell you?"

As justification, he criticized the verdict of these same jurors. He saw Brenda as a threat to society a laughable issue. Citing his earlier witnesses, he said, "You just can't find it."

Finally, Miskovsky stood before the jury, stating each of their names and said, "Do *not* mark death."

Attorney Fern Smith gave the state's final summation. "Brenda Andrew never shed a tear until it is about her...her daughter did not want to be here."

Smith reaffirmed that the law holds Brenda as equally guilty as her lover. She suggested mitigating circumstances.

"How does one mitigate a crime like this? There is no way to mitigate his death."

At the end of her statements, the jurors retired to establish Brenda's penalty.

Seven hours later, on Thursday, July 16, 2004, word flew throughout the courthouse that a decision was eminent. Brenda stood alongside her attorney while jurors filed into the room and were seated. The bailiff handed a paper to the judge. At that point, a cleaver would have split the tension. If I held my breath longer I'd launch an asthma attack or hyperventilate.

Judge Bragg looked at the paper and uttered one word, "Death." Before Brenda could show signs of a collapse, defense attorneys shielded her with their broad bodies, their arms encircling the shaking woman. They whisked her out the door into the defendant's chamber.

Handcuffed once more, she returned to the Oklahoma County Jail where she would await transfer to an interim facility at Lexington for mental and physical evaluation. From there she entered the next phase of her life on death row at the Mabel Bassett Correctional Facility in McCloud, Oklahoma. Elaborate remodeling was needed there to satisfy state requirements for housing the only woman serving the death sentence in Oklahoma.

Back in the courtroom, faces in the audience reflected the strain. Comforted by a relative, Rose Evers remained in the room long after most had shuffled into the hallway. Her family waved off media hounds with a brusque "No comment." A reasonable reaction.

Rob's brother, Tom, addressed reporters for the Andrew family. "Rob . . . surely has a favored seat at the right hand of God," he said. "The past two and a half years have been something we would not wish on our worst enemy."

CHAPTER 33

A New Home

Brenda Andrew joined ninety-seven death-row inmates. But she had the distinction of being the only *woman* given the death sentence.

Volunteers work in prison ministries hoping to bring small changes to wrecked lives. My limited experience working with Methodist prison ministries centered around baking cookies. Our study class provided sweet treats for inmates. We were restricted. Nuts, raisins, candies and coconut were not allowed. Incomprehensible, but these common ingredients might aid an escape.

My sensitivities did a one-eighty when I applied for an interview at Mabel Bassett Correctional Facility where Brenda was incarcerated. The possibility was remote that Brenda would grant me an audience. I had written to her in the County Jail but an elephant might access her with greater success. Throughout the trial her contempt for me was obvious. Letters to the Miskovsky firm had gone unanswered. I held but slight hope.

The internet provided limited information about Mabel Bassett. I went directly to the top. I wrote the warden a letter requesting a prison tour. My friend Carolyn Wall was at that time writing about the criminal justice system in Texas. She offered to go with me when the date was set. Following several phone calls from the Warden's Assistant, Liz Clayton, we settled on September 27, 2005. We allowed an hour for the drive to the prison.

McCloud, Oklahoma, is a wide spot in the road. Mile-markers outside the metropolitan area clicked into rolling hillsides east of

Oklahoma City. Cropland and pasture dominated the scene along Interstate 40. A lone sign marked the exit that led to life in a dimension beyond.

Road signs pointed to a turn off toward the prison. My chest tightened, signaling an asthma attack. To compensate, I inhaled deeply, slowly exhaling to retain oxygen. I glanced at Carolyn and wondered if she felt likewise, but she showed no anxiety. She'd been inside prisons in Texas.

Grey. My first impression was of dim block walls surrounded by endless spikey metallic rolls that glistened in the morning light. The guard tower, common to penal complexes, sat like a beacon on a lighthouse. I imagined eyes watching us from behind binoculars. I shuddered, certain my every move would be recorded.

We tossed jackets into the trunk and walked up the long sidewalk to the main gate. The gleaming razor wire rose before us, tiny knife-sharp barbs on coils of glistening cable rolled atop the fence surrounding the compound's entire perimeter. Another shudder came at the reality of the wire. These heavy barbs atop the fences completed the picture of a penal complex with no escape.

I pushed the buzzer on the front gate and waited. Time crept. A uniformed guard finally sauntered from the inside building to the gate.

"I need to know your names and business here," he said.

"I have an appointment with Mrs. Clayton the Assistant Warden for a prison tour." I tried to sound confident. Perhaps we weren't expected.

"Mrs. Clayton had a family emergency and isn't here today. I'm sorry but the warden is in a meeting. There's no one available to give tours."

Carolyn and I looked at one another. Deflated, I thanked the guard and asked, "When do you expect her back?"

"Call sometime next week," he said.

I waited a week and contacted Liz Clayton by e-mail. A second date was set for six weeks later.

Carolyn and I arrived at Mabel Bassett a second time. The morning was breezy with a chilly edge. Gloomy grey greeted us again, this stark place where my neighbor and once-friend would spend the rest of her life locked away.

This time we walked through heavy metal doors when Mrs. Clayton buzzed in an entry code. I surrendered my car keys and driver's license, the sole items allowed inside the gate. No jewelry, cameras, pencils or paper, cell phones or purses. We walked through a metal detector, footwear removed. We'd been told not to wear grey clothes because inmates were restricted to the drab color. Stepping back into our shoes, we entered a world unfamiliar to suburban grandmothers accustomed to Wal-Mart outings.

I held little hope of seeing Brenda Andrew but sneaked peeks at the pod housing high-security inmates. Not a soul was to be seen inside the fenced, dreary building. Walkways through a grassy area separated the four units. Clayton was a tiny lady but appeared respected by the inmates. An occasional seemingly friendly "Hi, Miz Clayton," echoed around us. However, one offender stepped in front of Clayton while we followed her on the walkway. The girl towered above the petite warden. The woman confronted Clayton in a tone that made my skin crawl. What had I gotten us into? The conversation concerned a minor misunderstanding. Unabashed, Clayton stood firm. Our walk resumed. Stares penetrated my back while I hurried to keep pace with Clayton. I was a bit scared of being left behind in the yard.

We skirted the chow hall. First lunch shift was in progress. The cafeteria could have been housed on a college campus instead of women's reformatory. That day, Carolyn and I were given the 'P.R' tour, the picture perfect, the best performance.

Clayton was proud that a select number of her inmates had achieved special status of wage earners. One room was filled with women taking telephone orders for goods manufactured within the Oklahoma Prison system. The activity mirrored that in any call center in the corporate world, a zone to which these workers might at some time return. Outside, they would earn more than the up-to-28 cents per hour made here. In the prison system, their earnings bought toilet items, soap, laundry needs and snack foods.

The dayroom was our next stop. Inside it, large windows allowed little privacy. Tables and chairs were bolted to the floor and a TV was anchored to the wall. An ice machine didn't work. Tables arranged in a U-shape completed a classroom next door. A large gymnasium provided ample exercise space. An enclosed outside yard was saturated with sunshine.

We entered one of four identical dormitory housing pods. Bunk beds in straight rows were bolted on a concrete floor. Inmates slept, read, stared at us or into space when we peered through a spacious viewing window. While we watched, one inmate covered her head with a sheet. We noticed a common unity of appearances: they were all young women with excessive makeup accented by heavy black eyeliner, crimped hairdos, either brassy blonde or coal black, and loose grey uniforms. A few girls waited for group therapy sessions, classes, lunch or physical activities. Others appeared totally bored.

Each narrow cell housed two girls. A bunk bed, one-piece toilet and small washbasin were the only fixtures. Each inmate had a shelf for toiletries and one wall hook for clothing. Each cell had one long, narrow window and a window in the steel door. A bank of switches outside controlled the lights in each cell, fitting for the medium security unit.

"Are the inmates in solitary housed like this?" I asked.

Clayton was reluctant to share the information.

"An inmate in solitary is in lock-down for twenty-three hours in her cell with no outside contact. One hour is allowed for exercise and to shower."

I concluded that Brenda's housing was similar to cells we had seen, the exception being her mandated solitude. She saw no one but her attorney through the glass and the guard who came to lead her to the shower.

Clayton indicated that an extensive remodeling to accommodate a death-row inmate was in progress. We guessed it included a chamber to carry out the death sentence. Maximum-security inmates were granted limited visitation, with those on a short list. Family members communicated by telephone through a glass wall, no physical touching tolerated. Clayton carefully avoided the restricted area where Andrew lived. I saw only the door through which she had passed.

Before leaving we viewed the visitation room in the front portion of the prison. Visitors had access to a small playroom behind a glass wall for accompanying children.

We re-entered the waiting area, relieved. I clutched my car keys when they were returned, my ticket to the outside world.

"Do you have photos of the facility for publicity purposes?" My question was rhetorical, but I had to ask.

"No," Clayton replied. "We don't allow photos here, for security reasons." She hesitated, but added in a near whisper, "I hear that one could get a good image from the McLoud cemetery across the hill."

I committed that information to my memory bank. I would come back another day.

Carolyn and I shared similar reactions to our penitentiary tour. True, girls there were offered some rehabilitation and job-skill opportunities. But how many would return to lives of crime once outside? We voiced our reflections into a tape recorder in a coffee shop in the nearby town of McLoud, afraid to lose thoughts and first impressions of Brenda Andrew's new home.

Two glaring realities struck us both. Not enough jobs were available to keep inmates busy. On the other hand, if life was really as good as painted at Mabel Bassett, what would be the incentive to leave?

The appeals process is a lengthy ordeal. Brenda's fate remains poised on the abilities of court-appointed attorneys who represent her case in the Court of Criminal Appeals. The entire process, if a sentence is upheld, can appear to crawl. The District Attorney confirmed that appeals can take up to ten or more years before final judgments are given.

I wonder, while sitting alone in her cell, what does Brenda think? Does she truly regret, or wish she had planned things differently?

CHAPTER 34

Life Goes On ...

Beginning with Rob's death late in 2001, reporters discovered new ways to cover the story. When Brenda, James and the children traveled in Mexico, *America's Most Wanted, Inside Edition* and *People Magazine* ran features about the bizarre killing. Dean and I collected reporters' business cards that were slipped between our doors.

Following the guilty verdicts, national players kept the coverage alive. Jupiter Entertainment interviewed us for a thirty-minute television show. *Snapped* was Jupiter's film short devoted to average women who commit crimes and the reasons why they had "snapped." The show would be aired on the Oxygen Channel, owned and sanctioned by Oprah Winfrey. The Jupiter team filmed Dean and me strolling the pathway through the greenbelt, demonstrating the escape route Pavatt had taken. Producers returned photos I had lent them, and gave us a DVD of the short project. Since the first airing on cable television, the Andrew *Snapped* story has been broadcast numerous times. Often, friends call us with the familiar line, "I just saw you on TV."

Conversely, Brenda's newspaper and TV coverage has been depressing. In October, 2004 Oklahoma County Judge Twyla Mason Gray granted Brenda indigent status. As a result Oklahoma taxpayers were burdened with the cost of her appeals. Brenda, by virtue of her diminished assets, now qualified for court-appointed legal representation throughout the appeals process. Among her possessions, the whereabouts of her hot tub were unknown, along with several pieces of jewelry. Dean chuckled about the missing hot tub, a major discussion point in his trial testimony. Assistant District Attorney Gieger said the tub was given to Brenda's sister, Kim Bowlin. Her costs covered by the state, Brenda was free to pursue her legal options.

Meanwhile, James Pavatt resided in the Oklahoma State Penitentiary at McAlister for a year prior to Brenda's conviction. Mike Arnett's firm had already begun Pavatt's appeals process. The major reason Pavatt refused to testify in Brenda's trial was to avoid compromising his own right to appeal. In April, 2008, the Oklahoma Court of Criminal Appeals rejected his appeal for post-conviction relief. At this writing, he may have additional appeals available.

The month of April, 2008 proved ominous for Brenda Andrew as well. In June, 2007 the Oklahoma Court of Criminal Appeals upheld her conviction and death sentence. Taking her case to the U.S. Supreme Court, attorneys argued that the trial judge improperly admitted certain evidence. They contended that the judge had prevented jurors from considering mitigating circumstances when reviewing facts for their death penalty decision. The Oklahoma Attorney General, who handles cases up for appeal, urged the highest court not to hear Brenda's appeal. Upon his recommendation, the U.S. Supreme Court refused to hear the case.

Both convicted killers sit on Death Row, the opportunities for conviction reversals or new trials looking bleak.

In a sad aftermath to Brenda's trial, her boisterous attorney, George Miskovsky III, has sustained legal problems of his own. On October 15, 2008 he pleaded guilty to two misdemeanor counts of offering to engage in acts of lewdness. Allegedly, he had sex with a fifteen-year-old girl at a hotel in April, 2005. He will lose his license to practice law and will serve 365 days in the Oklahoma County jail.

He has not been a member of Brenda Andrew's appeals legal team.

As for the Andrew children, the future appears brighter. They are surrounded by loving grandparents, by uncles, aunts and cousins who adore them. Understandably, the family has sheltered them from interviews. A faith-based school, positive environment, caring friends, and a nurturing religious structure and community will provide durable building blocks for the happiest and healthiest futures possible.

The house on Shaftsbury has undergone facelifts. Andrew's mother, Rose Evers arranged for its first transfer of ownership. The new owner, a small business man, had the necessary remodeling money at this disposal. Fresh paint, new light fixtures and plumbing, a near-white carpet and lightened woodwork achieved miracles. The outstanding accomplishment was an enclosure on the second floor, above the high-ceilinged living room, essentially creating an additional room. The extra 500 square feet could be used as a playroom or office.

I choked back tears when I toured the renovated house. Not long before, Rob had wanted an office in the house, to cut down on his traveling time and allow him more opportunity with his family. He had talked to us about an addition to the enclosed shed attached to the garage. A dream unfulfilled.

Before long, however, the house next door sat empty, the new owner anxious to sell it. Again, "For Sale" signs greeted us when entering our drive. Finally, a family with two young children bought the house and moved in. While it sat empty, Dean had mowed the meager grass that sprouted in the front yard. But real estate wheels turned and new neighbors moved in.

Early on, their invitations to an Easter Egg hunt included our grandchildren. The fun-loving couple, with polite, bright children, filled the former Andrew house with cheer. Family celebrations on the deck, friendly smiles and neighborly "hellos" brightened our cul-de-sac. Physically, the tragedy that engulfed us all has faded. Futures remain uncertain, but hope survives.

Rob Andrew did not live to celebrate that last Thanksgiving. But his children are held prayerfully in the hearts of those who knew them. May their future holidays be full of love for those who care for them and hold them dear.

The End

Made in the USA
Charleston, SC
07 January 2010